STUDY GUIDE

Christianity and Liberalism

Stephen J. Nichols

LIGONIER MINISTRIES
Renew your Mind.
LIGONIER.ORG | 800-435-4343

421 Ligonier Court, Sanford, FL 32771
E-mail: info@ligonier.org

Printed in China.

Contents

Introduction 3

Study Schedules 5

1 *The Present Emergency* 6

2 *The Life of J. Gresham Machen, Part 1* 14

3 *The Life of J. Gresham Machen, Part 2* 22

4 *Machen & the Church* 30

5 *Machen & Apologetics* 38

6 *Machen's Book* 46

7 *Doctrine* 53

8 *God & Man* 62

9 *The Bible* 70

10 *Christ* 77

11 *Salvation* 84

12 *The Church* 91

Introduction

In 1923, J. Gresham Machen wrote his classic work *Christianity and Liberalism*. Machen understood that he lived in a time that needed answers. People needed to know the fundamental doctrinal convictions of Christianity in an age of compromise. Modernism was threatening the church, and liberals within the church were seeking to accommodate it, calling into question bedrock doctrines of the faith. In this teaching series, Dr. Stephen J. Nichols reminds us of who Machen was, why his book is still important, and how it teaches us that there is only one true, uncompromising Christian faith.

This study guide is a companion to the video teaching series. Whether you are using the DVDs, streaming the videos on Ligonier.org, or going through the course in Ligonier Connect, this resource is designed to help you make the most of the learning experience. For each message in the series, there is a corresponding lesson in this guide. Here is what you will find in each lesson:

INTRODUCTION	The introduction is a brief paragraph that summarizes the content covered in the lecture and considered in the study guide lesson. **How to use:** Use the introduction to each lesson to get a sense of the big picture before watching the video. Refer to these statements as you work through the study guide to remind yourself of what you have already covered and where you are headed.
LEARNING GOALS	The learning goals are the knowledge and skills that the study guide lesson will endeavor to equip you with as you work through the lecture content. **How to use:** Familiarize yourself with the goals of each lesson before engaging its contents. Keeping the overall purpose in mind as you watch each video and reflect on or discuss the questions will help you get the most out of each lesson.
KEY IDEAS	The key ideas are the major points or takeaways from the lecture. **How to use:** Use these ideas to prepare yourself for each lesson and to review previous lessons. They describe specifically the knowledge that each lecture is communicating.

REFLECTION & DISCUSSION QUESTIONS	The questions are the guided reflection and/or discussion component of the lesson that is intended to help you prepare for, process, and organize what you are learning. **How to use:** Reflect on individually or discuss in a group the questions in the order in which they appear in the lesson. The time stamps in the right margin indicate where the answers to questions during the video can be found.
PRAYER	The prayer section offers suggestions for how to close the lesson in prayer with respect to what was taught in the lecture. **How to use:** Consider using each lesson's prayer section as a guide to personal or group prayer. These sections follow the ACTS prayer model, which you can learn more about in R.C. Sproul's Crucial Questions booklet *Does Prayer Change Things?* This helpful guide is available as a free e-book at Ligonier.org.
REVIEW QUIZ	The review quiz is a set of six multiple-choice questions that appears at the end of each lesson. **How to use:** Use each quiz to check your comprehension and memory of the major points covered in each lecture. It will be most beneficial to your learning if you take a lesson's quiz either sometime between lessons or just before you begin the next lesson in the study guide.
ANSWER KEY	The answer key provides explanations for the reflection and discussion questions and answers to the multiple-choice questions in the review quiz. **How to use:** Use the answer key to check your own answers or when you do not know the answer. Note: Do not give in too quickly; struggling for a few moments to recall an answer reinforces it in your mind.

Study Schedules

The following table suggests four plans for working through the *Christianity and Liberalism* video teaching series and this companion study guide. Whether you are going through this series on your own or with a group, these schedules should help you plan your study path.

	Extended 14-Week Plan	Standard 12-Week Plan	Abbreviated 6-Week Plan	Intensive 4-Week Plan
Week	**Lesson**			
1	*	1	1 & 2	1–3
2	1	2	3 & 4	4–6
3	2	3	5 & 6	7–9
4	3	4	7 & 8	10–12
5	4	5	9 & 10	
6	5	6	11 & 12	
7	6	7		
8	7	8		
9	8	9		
10	9	10		
11	10	11		
12	11	12		
13	12			
14	*			

* For these weeks, rather than completing lessons, spend your time discussing and praying about your learning goals for the study (the first week) and the most valuable takeaways from the study (the last week).

1

The Present Emergency

INTRODUCTION

"The Present Emergency and How to Meet It" was the title of the first radio recording in a series of talks from J. Gresham Machen to the American public. This message, when heard alongside his inaugural lecture as a professor at Princeton Theological Seminary, gives us a sense of Machen's unwavering convictions. In this lesson, Dr. Nichols explains how, despite change, Machen's answer to present emergencies was the Bible and its message.

LEARNING GOALS

When you have finished this lesson, you should be able to:

- Appreciate why undertaking this study on Machen and *Christianity and Liberalism* is relevant in the twenty-first century
- Explain the significance of Machen's central points in his radio program and inaugural lecture at Princeton Theological Seminary
- Summarize the pressing issues in the church and society at the time when Machen delivered these messages

KEY IDEAS

- The ultimate issue that people face, even amid worldly crisis, concerns their standing before God.
- Machen's response to crisis gives us perspective on our own crises as well as on their answer by keeping our eyes fixed on what is ultimate.

REFLECTION & DISCUSSION QUESTIONS

Before the Video

What Do You Think?

Take a moment to answer the following questions. They will prepare you for the lecture.

- What are the pressing present emergencies of today?

- What are your goals in undertaking this study on Machen and *Christianity and Liberalism*?

Scripture Reading

Jude, a servant of Jesus Christ and brother of James, to those who are called, beloved in God the Father and kept for Jesus Christ: May mercy, peace, and love be multiplied to you.

—Jude 1–2

- What realities in Jude's greeting before his call for us to contend for the faith assure us that our contending is not in vain?

During the Video

Answer the following questions while you watch the video. They will guide you through the lecture.

The Present Emergency *0:00–10:23*

- What motivated Machen to deliver his series of radio messages?

- What "present emergencies" did Machen call to mind in his first radio broadcast? What is the ultimate emergency?

The Inaugural Lecture *10:23–15:56*

- What did Machen assert about the church and modern culture in his inaugural lecture at Princeton Theological Seminary?

- How did Machen describe God in this inaugural lecture?

Ultimate Issues *15:56–24:19*

- What has the church needed to do since its beginning?

- What are some examples from church history that support Allan MacRae's statement about what the church has needed to do since its beginning?

After the Video

Answer the following questions after you have finished the lecture. They will help you identify and summarize the major points.

- Because Machen opened his broadcast with the various things that were causing people anxiety at that time, what can be concluded about Machen's character? Where does he direct people for answers?

  If you are in a group, ask the members the following questions: How can bringing to someone's mind what is truly ultimate help him or her through a tragedy or period of anxiety and worry? How can we do this without being dismissive of someone's experience?

- How was Machen's consistency in conveying the same message demonstrated in this lesson?

  If you are in a group, ask the members to share their list of present emergencies that they jotted down before the lecture and ask the following question: Is Machen's consistent message still relevant? How so?

- How might studying Machen's life and his work *Christianity and Liberalism* be helpful?

  If you are in a group, survey the members to see who might be interested in reading *Christianity and Liberalism* alongside this study.

PRAYER

Commit what you have learned from God's Word in this lesson to prayer.

- Praise God for His sovereign power that He displays through His acts of providence.
- Confess any doubts you might have about the ability of Scripture to answer today's problems.

- Thank God for faithful men and women throughout history who have remained steadfast for Christ.
- Ask God to increase your awareness of what is ultimate through this teaching series.

REVIEW QUIZ

Use these multiple-choice questions to measure what you learned from this lesson.

1. Which of the following was *not* one of the present emergencies that Machen brought to his audience's mind in "The Present Emergency and How to Meet It"?
   a. Modernism
   b. Unemployment
   c. The end of the gold standard
   d. The National Recovery Administration

2. Which statement summarizes Machen's main emphasis in "The Present Emergency and How to Meet It"?
   a. The advancement of Westminster Theological Seminary
   b. The everyday, tangible emergencies of society
   c. Modern culture's conflict with the Bible
   d. God and the unseen world

3. What did Machen consistently appeal to as the solution to the problems that he addressed throughout the messages in this lesson?
   a. Education
   b. Evangelism and missions
   c. The Bible as God's Word
   d. Mercy ministry

4. "The Present Emergency and How to Meet It" was the only message that Machen managed to broadcast before his death.
   a. True
   b. False

5. On what occasion was Machen's inaugural lecture at Princeton Theological Seminary?
   a. His becoming a first-time lecturer at the seminary
   b. His becoming a full-fledged professor at the seminary
   c. His becoming an assistant professor at the seminary
   d. His becoming an adjunct professor at the seminary

6. What is the church's "ceaseless struggle," according to Allan MacRae?
   a. "To combat modernism"
   b. "To advance the gospel"
   c. "To maintain the truth"
   d. "To remain pure"

Answer Key—The Present Emergency

REFLECTION & DISCUSSION QUESTIONS

Before the Video

What Do You Think?

These are personal questions. The answers should be based on your own knowledge and experience.

Scripture Reading

- What realities in Jude's greeting before his call upon us to contend for the faith assure us that our contending is not in vain?

  Jude opens his letter with the blessed truth that Christians are those who are "called," and this reality means that we are "beloved in God the Father and kept for Jesus Christ." This truth ought to assure us that our contending for the faith is not in vain. In our contending, it is natural for us to expect the results of Jude's blessing on the recipients of his letter: "mercy, peace, and love."

During the Video

The Present Emergency

- What motivated Machen to deliver his series of radio messages?

  While one of the trustees of Westminster Theological Seminary thought that Machen's appearance on the radio program would raise awareness and perhaps support for the seminary, Machen saw it as an opportunity to preach the gospel.

- What "present emergencies" did Machen call to mind in his first radio broadcast? What is the ultimate emergency?

  Machen mentioned three present emergencies to introduce what he considered to be the ultimate emergency. The first cause for alarm that people were then facing was the United States' moving away from the gold standard as the monetary system. Second, unemployment was still a reality only a few years after the Great Depression. Third, the National Recovery Administration was also on Americans' minds after the Great Depression. These perceived crises, however, were not the ultimate emergency in Machen's mind. The ultimate emergency is one's standing before God.

The Inaugural Lecture

- What did Machen assert about the church and modern culture in his inaugural lecture at Princeton Theological Seminary?

Machen pointed out that the world is fundamentally at odds with the Bible, and he also asserted that this fact has perplexed the church to such an extent that it would rather compromise than remain at odds. He alluded to the words of Jeremiah, who said that the unfaithful prophets and priests of Israel would cry, " 'Peace, Peace,' when there is no peace" (6:14).

- How did Machen describe God in this inaugural lecture?

  Machen's inaugural lecture as assistant professor highlighted his high view of God, contrasting Him with modernist views of God. Machen described God as a "mysterious, holy Person," who by His free grace sent forth His Son to deliver us from this world and into a relationship with Him.

Ultimate Issues

- What has the church needed to do since its beginning?

  Allan MacRae said in reference to Machen, "All through the history of the church, there has been a ceaseless struggle to maintain the truth." This reality is clearly seen in the New Testament in the ministries of such people as the Apostle Paul. Jude declared that we must "contend for the faith that was once for all delivered to the saints" (v. 3).

- What are some examples from church history that support Allan MacRae's statement about what the church has needed to do since its beginning?

  The church's struggle to maintain the truth can be immediately seen in the pages of the New Testament, and it can be seen in the church's writings throughout its history. The ecumenical creeds of the church were often formulated to defend the church against heresy. The Nicene and Chalcedonian Creeds are examples of this phenomenon. The great confessions that were born out of the Protestant Reformation also sought to maintain biblical truth.

After the Video

- Because Machen opened his broadcast with the various things that were causing people anxiety at that time, what can be concluded about Machen's character? Where does he direct people for answers?

  Machen brought to mind a number of things that were legitimately causing people concern at the time of his broadcast. He also acknowledged that in light of these things, "the world is weary and perplexed today." But he drove home the idea that the discontentment that people were facing was a matter of the soul. Machen cared about the souls of others and had great sympathy for people in their trouble, which is why he directed them to a true resource for help: the Bible.

- How was Machen's consistency in conveying the same message demonstrated in this lesson?

  Dr. Nichols surveyed three moments in Machen's life that spanned 1915 to 1935.

Over this twenty-year period, Machen maintained a consistent message that emphasized a reliance on the Word of God. In 1915 at his inaugural lecture as an assistant professor at Princeton Theological Seminary, he stressed the church's need to "decide for the Bible." In 1933, Machen echoed this conviction when he said, "The only place to stand is the Word of God." Finally, in his first radio broadcast in 1935, he appealed to his audience that the answers to the ultimate emergency that we all face are in "an old Book."

- How might studying Machen's life and his work *Christianity and Liberalism* be helpful?

  Machen's first radio message was titled "The Present Emergency and How to Meet It." No matter what time we find ourselves in, there will always be a present emergency. Studying Machen and his work can therefore give us perspective on our own emergencies and wisdom for how to answer them. The consistent message of his life can help us to keep our eyes on the things that are ultimate.

REVIEW QUIZ

1. **A.**
   The Great Depression was a severe economic crisis that resulted in the many anxieties that people faced in the 1930s, especially unemployment. The United States' move away from the gold standard and the National Recovery Administration were attempts to alleviate the dramatic economic downturn of the Great Depression. Modernism, a major concern for Machen, would not have been as prevalent in the minds of the American public.

2. **C.**
   Though Machen would particularly underscore modern culture's conflict with the Bible in his inaugural lecture at Princeton Theological Seminary, in this radio broadcast he explicitly identified "God and the unseen world" as the subject that he would be talking with his audience about.

3. **C.**
   The Bible indeed supports all these answers as necessary parts of the Christian life and perhaps solutions to a host of problems, but the one answer that underscores Machen's consistent message is the need to turn to the Bible as the authoritative Word of God.

4. **B.**
   "The Present Emergency and How to Meet It" was the first of fifty broadcasts that Machen aired from 1935 to 1937. The last of these messages were aired after his death on January 1, 1937.

5. **C.**
   Machen began serving Princeton Theological Seminary as a lecturer. The occasion for the inaugural lecture from this lesson, however, was his becoming assistant pro-

fessor of New Testament literature and exegesis.

6. **C.**
   MacRae, a student of Machen's, once said, "All through the history of the church, there has been a ceaseless struggle to maintain the truth." This idea is seen throughout church history and in the New Testament itself. The Apostles endeavored to prevent the spread of false teaching throughout the church and have called us to likewise contend for the faith.

2

The Life of J. Gresham Machen, Part 1

INTRODUCTION

Alongside the remarkable book *Christianity and Liberalism* is a remarkable life. The life of J. Gresham Machen twists and turns from a man who doesn't know what to do with his life to a man who would ultimately spend it in defending the Christian faith. In this lesson, Dr. Nichols divides Machen's life into four sections and explores the first two, "Foundations" and "Princeton I," describing Machen's well-to-do background and his journey toward Christian ministry.

LEARNING GOALS

When you have finished this lesson, you should be able to:

- Describe Machen's family life, early education, and college experience
- Summarize Machen's mentality and initial experience at Princeton Theological Seminary
- Explain the theological environment of the early twentieth century

KEY IDEAS

- The family that Machen was born into helped to provide him with an excellent education and formative encounters with some of the greatest texts of Western literature.
- Machen attended both Princeton University and Princeton Theological Seminary during a time when, though he was pursuing his genuine interests, he did not know exactly what he would do with his life.
- Machen excelled while at Princeton and continued part of his graduate work in Germany, where he encountered the German higher-critical tradition firsthand.

REFLECTION & DISCUSSION QUESTIONS

Before the Video

What Do You Think?

Take a moment to answer the following questions. They will prepare you for the lecture.

- What books have most shaped you?

- Have you ever experienced a season of life when you did not know what to do next? How did you decide on your course?

Scripture Reading

Listen to advice and accept instruction, that you may gain wisdom in the future. Many are the plans in the mind of a man, but it is the purpose of the LORD *that will stand.*

—Proverbs 19:20–21

- What does Scripture advise us to do when we do not know what to do next in our lives? Can you recall a moment in your life when you made a decision based on this scriptural wisdom?

During the Video

Answer the following questions while you watch the video. They will guide you through the lecture.

Foundations: 1881–1902 *0:00–13:17*

- What were the professions of Machen's father and his maternal and paternal grandfathers?

- What books influenced Machen as a young man? How does this connect to his major as an undergrad?

- Why was Machen initially reluctant to embrace the idea of seminary?

Princeton I: 1902–1918 *13:17–24:26*

- What degrees did Machen earn while at Princeton?
- What type of student was Machen at Princeton initially?
- After Germany, what did Machen return to Princeton to do? What was his next role at Princeton? What event interrupted Machen's life at Princeton during this season?

After the Video

Answer the following questions after you have finished the lecture. They will help you identify and summarize the major points.

- In what ways is Machen's uncertainty about what to do with his life seen in his years after college?

  If you are in a group, have the members discuss seasons of their lives when they did not know what to do. Ask: How have you found that God was at work even through these seasons of searching?
- How is Machen's brilliance seen throughout his academic career from Johns Hopkins to Princeton?

  If you are in a group, have each member discuss his or her impressions of Machen's upbringing and opportunities. Ask: In what ways is Machen relatable to you?
- What type of thinking did Machen encounter while in Germany? What did it attempt to undermine and how?

  If you are in a group, have the members discuss how questioning the Bible's statements about its authorship and its testimony to the supernatural undermines the whole of the Christian faith. Ask: What is lost if we question the historicity of the Bible?

PRAYER

Commit what you have learned from God's Word in this lesson to prayer.

- Praise God for His wisdom in orchestrating the details of our lives.

- Confess any areas in which you are not leaning on the Lord's understanding for guidance.
- Thank God for the many undeserved blessings that you enjoy in this life.
- Ask God to give you an excellent diligence in learning about Him.

REVIEW QUIZ

Use these multiple-choice questions to measure what you learned from this lesson.

1. Where was Machen born?
   a. Baltimore
   b. Philadelphia
   c. Pittsburgh
   d. Macon

2. Who wrote detective stories for financial support through school?
   a. Machen's mother
   b. Machen's maternal grandfather
   c. Machen's paternal grandfather
   d. Machen's father

3. Which U.S. president did Machen often dine with?
   a. Theodore Roosevelt
   b. William Howard Taft
   c. Woodrow Wilson
   d. Calvin Coolidge

4. Which profession made seminary sound like a strange choice for Machen?
   a. Banker
   b. Lawyer
   c. Pastor
   d. Scholar

5. Machen served as an Army chaplain in World War I.
   a. True
   b. False

6. What distinction were the German theologians of Machen's day attempting to make?
   a. The distinction between different authorial strands of the Pentateuch
   b. The distinction between biblical inerrancy and biblical infallibility
   c. The distinction between the Jesus of history and the Jesus of faith
   d. The distinction between logical and temporal priority in soteriology

Answer Key—The Life of J. Gresham Machen, Part 1

REFLECTION & DISCUSSION QUESTIONS

Before the Video

What Do You Think?

These are personal questions. The answers should be based on your own knowledge and experience.

Scripture Reading

- What does Scripture advise us to do when we do not know what to do next in our lives? Can you recall a moment in your life when you made a decision based on this scriptural wisdom?

  The wise advice of Scripture, echoed throughout Proverbs, is that we are to also seek out advice from others. We need to be in a posture of humble acceptance when it comes to the advice and instruction of others, especially when we do not know what to do about the future.

During the Video

Foundations: 1881–1902

- What were the professions of Machen's father and his maternal and paternal grandfathers?

  Each of these men worked in the judicial field. Machen's maternal grandfather was a lawyer and president of the board of trustees of the University of Georgia. Machen's paternal grandfather was the chief law clerk for the United States Senate. Machen's father, who supported himself through law school at Harvard by writing detective stories, was also a lawyer.

- What books influenced Machen as a young man? How does this connect to his major as an undergrad?

  Machen was influenced by the Bible, Bunyan's The Pilgrim's Progress, *and the Westminster Shorter Catechism. His mother loved the Bible and Victorian culture, even publishing a book titled* The Bible in Browning. *His father collected Greek and Latin classics, and access to these classics greatly influenced Machen. He would major in classics at Johns Hopkins University.*

- Why was Machen initially reluctant to embrace the idea of seminary?

  Machen was guided by his pastor to consider seminary in light of his interests and abilities, but he did not want to be a pastor. In this sense, seminary was the last thing on his mind, but his pastor encouraged him that he could go to seminary and become a scholar instead, even attending university while at seminary.

Princeton I: 1902–1918

- What degrees did Machen earn while at Princeton?

  Machen attended both Princeton University and Princeton Theological Seminary. Through the university, he received a master of arts in philosophy; through the seminary, he received a bachelor of divinity, which is equivalent to a master of divinity today.

- What type of student was Machen at Princeton initially?

  Because Machen was brilliant, he often did not have to apply himself. He became consumed with Princeton football and would even skip class to attend games. As evidenced by the school notebooks that we have from Machen, he often joked with classmates. Machen himself acknowledged that during this period he was "playing games."

- After Germany, what did Machen return to Princeton to do? What was his next role at Princeton? What event interrupted Machen's life at Princeton during this season?

  After Machen returned from studying abroad, he became a lecturer at Princeton in 1906. He did not immediately pursue ordination, but he would eventually become ordained and serve as the assistant professor of New Testament for the seminary in 1915. World War I began in 1914, and Machen wanted to serve, so he went to the front lines with the YMCA to provide services to American soldiers.

After the Video

- In what ways is Machen's uncertainty about what to do with his life seen in his years after college?

  After Machen graduated from college, his parents sent him on a tour of Europe, where he fell in love with hiking the Alps. Upon his return, he still did not know what he wanted to do. His brothers were set on becoming lawyers, and Machen also entertained becoming a lawyer and explored the idea of becoming a banker, even taking a semester to study international banking at the University of Chicago. He would eventually ask for guidance from his pastor, who directed him to Princeton.

- How is Machen's brilliance seen throughout his academic career from Johns Hopkins to Princeton?

  While at Johns Hopkins, Machen won a senior prize and became valedictorian of his class. He would go on to attend both Princeton University and Princeton Theological Seminary, earning degrees from both institutions simultaneously.

While studying at Princeton, he was able to do well even with a divided focus. As a senior, however, he wrote a paper that earned him a full year of graduate study abroad in Germany.

- What type of thinking did Machen encounter while in Germany? What did it attempt to undermine and how?

  While in Germany, Machen encountered German higher criticism firsthand. In the nineteenth century, questions of biblical authorship were being rigorously explored, and the documentary hypothesis, also known as the JEDP theory, was posited. It asserted that the Pentateuch had not been written by Moses but had been pulled together from multiple authorial strands, each with its unique theological emphases. This same type of thinking was later applied to the Gospels as scholars attempted to sort out the difference between a historical Jesus and a Jesus of myth and legend who had supposedly been created by the Christian community. Both ideas attack the historicity and divine inspiration of the Bible.

REVIEW QUIZ

1. **A.**
   The Gresham family, Machen's maternal side, had deep ties in Georgia. Machen's mother was from Macon, and his grandfather even served as the president on the board of trustees of the University of Georgia. Machen, however, was born in Baltimore, Md.

2. **D.**
   Arthur Webster Machen, Machen's father, determined to support himself through law school, and he did so by writing detective novels. Machen's mother, Mary, was also a published author, having written a work on the poet Elizabeth Barrett Browning and the Bible.

3. **C.**
   Each served as president of the United States during Machen's lifetime, and Machen often dined with Woodrow Wilson, who was a family friend and president of Princeton University before he became U.S. president.

4. **C.**
   Machen had no desire to become a lawyer or a banker, which is one of the reasons that his pastor suggested seminary. But Machen thought of seminary only in terms of becoming a pastor, which also did not appeal to him. The thought of becoming a scholar, however, did ultimately appeal to him.

5. **B.**
   Though Machen initially considered serving as a chaplain, he understood that chaplaincy would somewhat remove him from the troops. To be closer to the troops, Machen served with the YMCA, providing various social services on the front lines.

6. **C.**
Machen studied in Germany for a time. This period was influenced by previous German schools of thought, such as those that conceived of the JEDP theory of how the Pentateuch had developed. The same line of thinking shaped how scholars in Machen's day approached the Gospels in an attempt to distinguish between the historical Jesus (who Jesus really was in history) and the Jesus of faith (the mythical figure created by early Christians).

3

The Life of J. Gresham Machen, Part 2

INTRODUCTION

It may be surprising to learn that J. Gresham Machen met with much adversity later in his life. He faced challenges both at Princeton and denominationally, leading Machen to form a new seminary and Presbyterian denomination. In this lesson, Dr. Nichols concludes his survey of Machen's life, describing how Machen remained faithful to his life calling and work in service to Christ as a scholar and churchman.

LEARNING GOALS

When you have finished this lesson, you should be able to:

- Describe Machen's relationship with B.B. Warfield
- Identify key turning points in Machen's life at Princeton
- Explain the issues that led Machen to form a new theological seminary and denomination

KEY IDEAS

- World War I gave Machen a richer understanding of Scripture and a deeper resolve about his purpose in life once he returned to Princeton.
- Machen's mentor B.B. Warfield helped him to see the state of disrepair in the Presbyterian denomination.
- Progressives began to dominate the board of Princeton Theological Seminary to the point that Machen saw the need for a new seminary, and issues over foreign missions culminated in Machen's founding a new denomination entirely.

REFLECTION & DISCUSSION QUESTIONS

Before the Video

What Do You Think?

Take a moment to answer the following questions. They will prepare you for the lecture.

- Why is it important that seminaries be faithful to the truth of God's Word?
- What is the purpose of foreign missions?

Scripture Reading

I appeal to you, brothers, by the name of our Lord Jesus Christ, that all of you agree, and that there be no divisions among you, but that you be united in the same mind and the same judgment.

—1 Corinthians 1:10

- In light of this verse, what's important to consider when thinking about church splits and the forming of new denominations?

During the Video

Answer the following questions while you watch the video. They will guide you through the lecture.

Princeton II *0:00–13:44*

- What two key events helped Machen find his purpose in life?
- What did Machen share in common with B.B. Warfield?
- What did Machen say at Warfield's memorial service? How did this sentiment come to fruition at Princeton Theological Seminary?

New Wineskins *13:44–24:20*

- What did Machen do in response to the changes at Princeton Theological Seminary? Why is this important for the life of the church?

- What did the study "Re-thinking Missions" assert?

- What precipitated Machen's forming of a new Presbyterian denomination?

After the Video

Answer the following questions after you have finished the lecture. They will help you identify and summarize the major points.

- How is Machen's exchange with Warfield about the state of the Presbyterian denomination helpful for processing division in the church?

  If you are in a group, have the members read 1 Corinthians 11:17–19 and ask: Though division in the church is a sad reality, in what ways might it sometimes be necessary? How might it be helpful?
- Why is it surprising that Machen's nomination and appointment to become the professor of apologetics was rejected and denied?

  If you are in a group, have the members discuss what ought to be determinative in nominations within the church to offices such as elder and deacon.
- Why was Machen not, in actuality, in violation of his ordination vows when acting on the state of foreign missions in his denomination?

  If you are in a group, have the members do a thought experiment that attempts to describe what missions would be like without evangelism.

PRAYER

Commit what you have learned from God's Word in this lesson to prayer.

- Praise God for the Spirit of unity who is shared between believers.
- Confess any unnecessary division you might have between yourself and another Christian.
- Thank God that Jesus Christ has promised the church's preservation.
- Ask God to give you a heart for unity and truth.

REVIEW QUIZ

Use these multiple-choice questions to measure what you learned from this lesson.

1. What is a common thread in Machen's wartime letters that were read in this lesson?
   a. Courage
   b. Disillusionment
   c. Political reflection
   d. Thanksgiving
2. What chapter of Scripture did Machen truly understand after World War I?
   a. Genesis 3
   b. Psalm 23
   c. Romans 8
   d. Hebrews 11
3. B.B. Warfield believed that a split was necessary to save Presbyterianism.
   a. True
   b. False
4. What was *not* something that Machen held in common with Warfield?
   a. Both loved Greek and Latin classics
   b. Both were New Testament professors
   c. Both had family members who had written books
   d. Both were professors of apologetics at Princeton
5. Machen's report on the "Re-thinking Missions" study was heavily analyzed by his presbytery.
   a. True
   b. False
6. All but which of the following events happened before the founding of Westminster Theological Seminary?
   a. Death of B.B. Warfield
   b. Publication of "Re-thinking Missions" study
   c. Founding of the Orthodox Presbyterian Church
   d. Reorganization of Princeton's board of directors

Answer Key—The Life of J. Gresham Machen, Part 2

REFLECTION & DISCUSSION QUESTIONS

Before the Video

What Do You Think?

These are personal questions. The answers should be based on your own knowledge and experience.

Scripture Reading

- In light of this verse, what's important to consider when thinking about church splits and the forming of new denominations?

  In this letter to the Corinthians, the Apostle Paul clearly condemns all forms of division in the church, but he also calls the church to be unified in its thinking and judgments. When truth is jeopardized in the church, such unity of mind may become impossible between Christians, leading to justifiable splits on a denominational level.

During the Video

Princeton II

- What two key events helped Machen find his purpose in life?

  The first event spans Machen's experience in World War I. As can be seen in his letters, his experience was formative in his understanding of Scripture and true thanksgiving to God. The second event was the death of his mentor B.B. Warfield.

- What did Machen share in common with B.B. Warfield?

  Like Warfield, Machen loved the Greek and Latin classics, and he also had the same scholarly aptitude. After being a lecturer at Princeton Theological Seminary, Machen became a New Testament professor, the same position that Warfield began at Western Theological Seminary. Warfield would become the professor of apologetics at Princeton, a position to which Machen would also be nominated.

- What did Machen say at Warfield's memorial service? How did this sentiment come to fruition at Princeton Theological Seminary?

  As people carried Warfield's body out of Miller Chapel, Machen said, "They are carrying Old Princeton with him." Princeton Theological Seminary was changing, and though Machen was the new champion of orthodoxy, he could not stop the change altogether. In fact, Machen's nomination to be professor of apologetics at

Princeton was rejected and denied by the Presbyterian Church's General Assembly, and the board at Princeton was reorganized such that conservatives could not possibly carry a majority vote in future seminary decisions.

New Wineskins

- What did Machen do in response to the changes at Princeton Theological Seminary? Why is this important for the life of the church?

  After being rejected as the professor of apologetics and after seeing the writing on the wall in the reorganization of Princeton's board, Machen struck out and founded a new theological seminary, Westminster Theological Seminary. As concerns the life of the church, seminaries provide the pastors to fill the pulpits and preach to God's people, so a new confessional seminary would work to preserve confessional, orthodox preaching.

- What did the study "Re-thinking Missions" assert?

  The study of a Harvard professor, "Re-thinking Missions" was published in 1933. It studied mission agencies of six denominations and their work in such places as India, China, and Japan. It concluded that missions should no longer be focused on proselytization and evangelism but should be focused on the physical health and well-being of others.

- What precipitated Machen's forming of a new Presbyterian denomination?

  Machen could not abide the new paradigm of missions that was sweeping through his denomination. He denounced the practices of the current missionary board of his denomination, and he set up a new missionary board for those who wanted to faithfully proclaim the gospel. These actions were deemed a violation of his ordination vows. So in 1936, Machen and 120 ruling and teaching elders formed the Orthodox Presbyterian Church.

After the Video

- How is Machen's exchange with Warfield about the state of the Presbyterian denomination helpful for processing division in the church?

  Machen, conversing with Warfield, likened the denomination to dead wood in light of the rise of liberalism within it. Machen sensed that a split was on the horizon, but Warfield replied, "You can't split dead wood." Warfield understood that the denomination was probably too far gone. This helps us to assess division in the church with some nuance, realizing that not all division is created equal and that it is sometimes necessary.

- Why is it surprising that Machen's nomination and appointment to become the professor of apologetics was rejected and denied?

  Machen seemed to be the next Warfield. It would have been natural for him to also become the professor of apologetics at Princeton. Machen had also recently published Christianity and Liberalism and was seen to be the defender of orthodoxy. On this account alone, the rejection and denial of his appointment to this position was surprising, but what made it even more surprising was that such nominations were typically rubber-stamped at the General Assembly level.

- Why was Machen not, in actuality, in violation of his ordination vows when acting on the state of foreign missions in his denomination?

  Machen's report against "Re-thinking Missions" and particularly his setting up the Independent Board of Presbyterian Foreign Missions were deemed to violate his ordination vows, as if he were siphoning off funds from the denominational board. This denominational board was engaging in missionary practices in step with "Re-thinking Missions" and thus not sharing the gospel. In a very real sense, Machen was actually upholding his ordination vows as a gospel minister by promoting missions that were in accord with the heart of the Great Commission.

REVIEW QUIZ

1. **D.**
   Far from being disillusioned, believing that God would sustain his courage, Machen wrote letter after letter that emphasized his thanksgiving to the Lord. On a lighter note, he recounted his "prayer of thanksgiving" after finding a pair of dry socks. He also described his understanding of "true thanksgiving" after the war came to an end.

2. **C.**
   Romans 8 describes the manifold realities in this life that we would think could separate us from the love of God in Christ but, in actuality, can't. Nothing can separate us from God's love in Christ. Machen learned this truth firsthand in his being preserved during World War I.

3. **B.**
   Machen entertained the idea that a split in the denomination was on the horizon, but Warfield did not think a split was possible. In response to Machen's likening Presbyterianism to a tree, Warfield said, "You can't split dead wood."

4. **D.**
   Machen held all these things in common with his mentor B.B. Warfield except having been a professor of apologetics at Princeton Theological Seminary. Machen's nomination and appointment for this position was rejected and denied, but he would become the professor of apologetics at Westminster Theological Seminary.

5. **B.**
   Machen's report against the "Re-thinking Missions" study was extensive, yet it was not taken seriously. A vote on the report was not even brought to the floor of presbytery. It was largely ignored.

6. **C.**
   All these events happened before the forming of Westminster Theological Seminary except the organization of the Orthodox Presbyterian Church on June 11, 1936, only six months before Machen's untimely death.

4

Machen & the Church

INTRODUCTION

J. Gresham Machen was a churchman. He cared deeply for Christ's church and was zealous for its health. For this reason, he did not avoid controversy and conflict over the essentials of the Christian faith even though he did not seek it out. In this lesson, Dr. Nichols explains why conflict and controversy are sometimes necessary and how Machen promoted conviction and clarity in the church.

LEARNING GOALS

When you have finished this lesson, you should be able to:

- Appreciate Machen's integrity in times of controversy and conflict
- Recognize how shrinking from controversy and conflict is not foundationally biblical
- Explain the historical moments that shaped Machen's life in the church

KEY IDEAS

- Machen said, "Controversy and conflict bring clarity and conviction."
- After Princeton Theological Seminary lost its bearings, Machen founded Westminster Theological Seminary to be a place of "solid learning" to train specialists in the Bible.
- In the inaugural sermon of the Orthodox Presbyterian Church, Machen underscored the importance of the church of Jesus Christ's being a confessional church.

REFLECTION & DISCUSSION QUESTIONS

Before the Video

What Do You Think?

Take a moment to answer the following questions. They will prepare you for the lecture.

- What do conflict and controversy typically lead to, in your experience? Why?

- Why do we have creeds, catechisms, and confessions in the church?

Scripture Reading

If you put these things before the brothers, you will be a good servant of Christ Jesus, being trained in the words of the faith and of the good doctrine that you have followed. Have nothing to do with irreverent, silly myths. Rather train yourself for godliness; for while bodily training is of some value, godliness is of value in every way, as it holds promise for the present life and also for the life to come. The saying is trustworthy and deserving of full acceptance. For to this end we toil and strive, because we have our hope set on the living God, who is the Savior of all people, especially of those who believe.

—1 Timothy 4:6–10

- How are churches and Christian educational institutions such as seminaries and Bible colleges to remain faithful, in light of these verses?

During the Video

Answer the following questions while you watch the video. They will guide you through the lecture.

Clarity and Conviction *0:00–8:33*

- How did Machen answer the criticism that he always seemed to be focusing on the negative?

- Why is Athanasius a good analogue to Machen?

Machen and the Seminary *8:33–17:32*

- What had Princeton Theological Seminary once stood for, according to Machen?

- Why was Machen concerned about the direction of Princeton Theological Seminary?

Machen, Missions, and Confession *17:32–25:07*

- How did Pearl Buck describe her frustration with missions?

- What was Machen's sermon text at the second General Assembly of the Orthodox Presbyterian Church? What did Machen stress in this sermon?

After the Video

Answer the following questions after you have finished the lecture. They will help you identify and summarize the major points.

- Why would someone get the impression that Machen was contentious? Why is this a misconception?

  If you are in a group, have the members consider how standing up for truth might affect an ordinary Christian's life. Ask: What are some arenas in which it is difficult for a Christian to stand for the truth?

- Why is education important for ministers of the gospel?

  If you are in a group, have the members discuss their answers to the questions above. Ask: Are educational credentials alone enough for faithfulness in ministry? What else is necessary?

- How could Machen have been so bold as to talk about the privilege of writing the Westminster Standards "in patient instruction by the blessing of the Holy Spirit upon the tablets of our children's hearts"?

  If you are in a group, have the members discuss why it may be that the church has moved away from catechesis of children and adults alike.

PRAYER

Commit what you have learned from God's Word in this lesson to prayer.

- Praise God for His power, knowing that nothing can thwart His will.

- Confess ways that you struggle to stand on the conviction of God's powerful Word.
- Thank God for the powerful preservation of His Word throughout history and the church's remaining steadfast to its truth.
- Ask God to use you through the power of His Spirit to faithfully share His Word with others and pass it down to future generations.

REVIEW QUIZ

Use these multiple-choice questions to measure what you learned from this lesson.

1. How was Princeton Theological Seminary initially structured?
   a. With a president who oversaw major decisions
   b. With a large board that oversaw institutional and theological concerns
   c. With two boards, one that oversaw institutional decisions and one that oversaw curricula and faculty decisions
   d. With a single board of trustees to promote the seminary
2. Machen was not afraid of conflict and actively sought it out.
   a. True
   b. False
3. What is *not* one of the answers given to the criticism that Machen's teaching was reactionary and negative?
   a. Paying attention to the institutes that train ministers is vital for the health of the church
   b. Avoiding argument is not characteristic of the Christianity of the New Testament
   c. Examining false gospels sharpens one's understanding of the true gospel
   d. Allowing false teaching to go unchecked is unloving to others
4. What word did Machen use to describe the people whom Westminster Theological Seminary trained?
   a. Academics
   b. Experts
   c. Scholars
   d. Specialists
5. *Confessional* summarizes Machen's desire for the church.
   a. True
   b. False
6. What word did Machen repeat to great rhetorical effect in his sermon at the second General Assembly of the Orthodox Presbyterian Church?
   a. Clarity
   b. Conviction
   c. Privilege
   d. Truth

Answer Key—Machen & the Church

REFLECTION & DISCUSSION QUESTIONS

Before the Video

What Do You Think?

These are personal questions. The answers should be based on your own knowledge and experience.

Scripture Reading

- How are churches and Christian educational institutions such as seminaries and Bible colleges to remain faithful, in light of these verses?

  One phrase that is important to notice is "the faith." The Christian faith has objective content that does not change, such that it is often referred to as "the faith." This is the same phrase that Jude used when he said, "Contend for the faith" (v. 3). The very thing that Timothy is to put before others is the content of the faith that he has received. Likewise, for churches and educational institutions to remain faithful, they must also hand down this faith, and this will bear the fruit of godliness and salvation.

During the Video

Clarity and Conviction

- How did Machen answer the criticism that he always seemed to be focusing on the negative?

  Machen challenged false beliefs, and he often did so in the classroom, such that the criticism arose that his work at Princeton was characteristically negative. He replied, "All our examination of objections to the gospel is employed only as a means to lead men to a clearer understanding of what the gospel is and to a clearer and more triumphant conviction of its truth."

- Why is Athanasius a good analogue to Machen?

  Like Machen, Athanasius stood for truth and found himself in the throes of conflict. He stood for the church's true teaching concerning the person of Christ. As a result, however, he was removed from his bishopric.

Machen and the Seminary

- What had Princeton Theological Seminary once stood for, according to Machen?

Not only did Machen understand that the seminary's foundation on which it stood was the Word of God and its truthfulness, but he also recognized that Reformed theology is the system of doctrine that God's Word teaches. The seminary had been faithful to these convictions for over one hundred years, but Machen saw that things were changing.

- Why was Machen concerned about the direction of Princeton Theological Seminary?

  Machen had an unwavering integrity and desire to see the truth of God's Word taught in the seminary because he understood that if the seminary departed from the truth, then the denomination would not be far behind. As Dr. Nichols said, "As goes the seminary, so goes the denomination."

Machen, Missions, and Confession

- How did Pearl Buck describe her frustration with missions?

  Buck, a daughter of medical missionaries to China, once said, "I am weary unto death with this incessant preaching." The trend in missiology during Machen's time was to place the emphasis of missions on mercy ministry apart from the preaching of the Word. Buck's sentiment captures this trend.

- What was Machen's sermon text at the second General Assembly of the Orthodox Presbyterian Church? What did Machen stress in this sermon?

  Machen preached from 2 Corinthians 5:14–15 on the constraining love of Jesus Christ. In a rhetorical flourish, he stressed how privileged the church is to have been given the message of the gospel to proclaim throughout the world and from one generation to the next—the latter particularly through the Westminster Standards.

After the Video

- Why would someone get the impression that Machen was contentious? Why is this a misconception?

  In the 1920s and 1930s, Machen seemed to be embroiled in controversy. Machen's being rejected as a professor of apologetics and being removed from his denomination make one ask whether he was looking for trouble. The truth is that when one stands for the truth, controversy and conflict are inevitable. This is why B.B. Warfield understood that "the cool closets of the scholar's reflection" are not for men such as Machen and anyone else who stands for truth.

- Why is education important for ministers of the gospel?

  As already stated, "As goes the seminary, so goes the denomination." Dr. Nichols also remarked further about Machen's desires for Westminster Theological Seminary to produce specialists in the Bible. We live in a world that prizes education, which is required for many professions, and so it is understandable why education is also important for ministers of the gospel. Only if ministers are knowledgeable will they have the ability to answer difficult questions for God's people.

- How could Machen have been so bold as to talk about the privilege of writing the Westminster Standards "in patient instruction by the blessing of the Holy Spirit upon the tablets of our children's hearts"?

  It may be surprising to hear such bold language about the Westminster Standards because the language is evocative of one of the promises of the new covenant in the writing of God's law upon the hearts of His people. Machen said this, however, in the full conviction that the Westminster Standards are a truthful summary of God's Word.

REVIEW QUIZ

1. **C.**
   Initially, Princeton Theological Seminary did not have a president, and it was run by two boards, a board of directors and a board of trustees. The board of directors maintained control of decisions over matters such as faculty and curricula, which would guide the theological framework of the institution. The board of trustees oversaw financial and facility decisions for the ordinary care of the seminary.

2. **B.**
   While it is true that Machen was not afraid of and did not shy away from conflict, he did not actively seek it out. It is a misconception to view Machen, on account of the controversies that he became embroiled in, as a curmudgeon. He was a churchman who cared about the faithfulness of Christ's church.

3. **D.**
   We ought to affirm the truth that false teaching must be challenged. One reason is that false teaching jeopardizes another's soul, so it would be unloving both to the false teacher and to his or her listeners if false teaching was not challenged. This concept, however, was not one of Machen's emphases as to why examining opposing views is necessary, though it is an implication to be drawn from his points.

4. **D.**
   In Machen's inaugural address at Westminster Theological Seminary, he said, "We will train specialists in the Bible." Just as a medical school trains specialists in medicine and a law school trains specialists in the law, a seminary ought to train specialists in the Bible.

5. **A.**
   Machen desired a confessional church. Confessions define and animate the church, and they give the church a solid understanding of the truth and what it should be teaching in line with that truth. Apart from them, a church can all too easily veer from the truth.

6. **C.**

   Again and again, Machen used the word privilege *in his sermon to drive home how privileged the church is to have been given the gospel to proclaim. One example of this from his sermon: "What a privilege to carry the message of the cross, unshackled by compromising association to the world!"*

5

Machen & Apologetics

INTRODUCTION

Apologetics is the defense of the Christian faith, and it was crucially important to J. Gresham Machen. He dedicated his scholarly output to defending essential points of the faith against modernistic reinterpretations. In this lesson, Dr. Nichols defines apologetics and Machen's approach to apologetics, underscoring its role in exposing error and preserving the gospel as well as its role in bolstering our faith.

LEARNING GOALS

When you have finished this lesson, you should be able to:

- Define apologetics and its purpose
- Explain how the New Testament is itself an apologetic and calls us to do apologetics
- Summarize Machen's approach toward apologetics and some defining features of classical apologetics

KEY IDEAS

- Apologetics is the reasoned defense of the Christian faith and its content.
- The New Testament calls Christians to the task of apologetics, which is essential to the very nature of the New Testament itself.
- Machen took a classical approach to apologetics, believing that apologetics should start with arguments for God's existence.

REFLECTION & DISCUSSION QUESTIONS

Before the Video

What Do You Think?

Take a moment to answer the following questions. They will prepare you for the lecture.

- Why is it important to know what you believe and why you believe it?

- What is the most difficult thing about sharing your faith with others?

Scripture Reading

Now who is there to harm you if you are zealous for what is good? But even if you should suffer for righteousness' sake, you will be blessed. Have no fear of them, nor be troubled, but in your hearts honor Christ the Lord as holy, always being prepared to make a defense to anyone who asks you for a reason for the hope that is in you; yet do it with gentleness and respect, having a good conscience, so that, when you are slandered, those who revile your good behavior in Christ may be put to shame. For it is better to suffer for doing good, if that should be God's will, than for doing evil.

—1 Peter 3:13–17

- In what context does Peter especially call us to be prepared to defend our faith?

During the Video

Answer the following questions while you watch the video. They will guide you through the lecture.

Apologetics and Machen's Approach *0:00–13:16*

- What is the meaning of the Greek words that make up the English word *apologetics*?

- What is often the context for the word *apologia* in the New Testament? What is the apologetic message of the New Testament?

- In step with a classical approach to apologetics, where does Machen begin his apologetic arguments for the Christian faith?

Apologetics for the Church, Culture, and You *13:16–24:33*

- How were liberal theologians distorting the gospel in the church? What was one of Machen's responses to this type of distortion?

- What did Machen believe that modernism was creating in human life and culture?

- In what sense is apologetics for the Christian?

After the Video

Answer the following questions after you have finished the lecture. They will help you identify and summarize the major points.

- How does the New Testament call Christians to the task of apologetics?

  If you are in a group, have the members discuss their experiences with defending the faith with unbelievers. Ask: What was effective and ineffective in these experiences?

- What is the order of Machen's apologetics?

  If you are in a group, have the members discuss any strengths or weaknesses in taking this approach to apologetics.

- Why did Machen believe it was important to write a scholarly work on the virgin birth of Jesus Christ?

  If you are in a group, have the members name events that are critical to the message of the gospel. Ask: Can the truth claims of Christianity be sustained apart from their historical validity? Why or why not?

PRAYER

Commit what you have learned from God's Word in this lesson to prayer.

- Praise God for sending His Son into the world to save it.
- Confess ways that you fail in your responsibility to share the gospel or to share it winsomely.
- Thank God for the numerous examples in Scripture of faith through challenging

circumstances.

- Ask God to grant you by His Spirit the desire to honor Christ in how you live and how you witness to others even when reviled.

REVIEW QUIZ

Use these multiple-choice questions to measure what you learned from this lesson.

1. Which of the following was *not* provided as an example of someone's giving an *apologia* in a trial context?
   a. Jesus in the gospel of Luke
   b. The Apostles in the book of Acts
   c. Paul in his letter to the Philippians
   d. Socrates in Athens in 399 BC

2. Machen said, "We do not indeed begin with the conviction that the Bible is the Word of God in our defense of the Christian religion."
   a. True
   b. False

3. What is the order of Machen's apologetics as it relates to the Bible?
   a. The supernatural origin of the Bible proves the historicity of the Bible, which proves the authoritative nature of the Bible as the Word of God.
   b. The authoritative nature of the Bible as the Word of God proves the historicity of the Bible, which proves the supernatural origin of the Bible.
   c. The historicity of the Bible, which attests to its supernatural origins, proves the authoritative nature of the Bible as the Word of God.
   d. The historicity of the Bible assumes the authoritative nature of the Bible as God's Word, which explains its supernatural origin.

4. The denial of the virgin birth obscures the nature of Jesus' death.
   a. True
   b. False

5. In denying the historicity of the resurrection, liberal theologians were in effect denying what critical passage on the resurrection, according to Dr. Nichols?
   a. Matthew 28
   b. Romans 6
   c. 1 Corinthians 15
   d. Revelation 20

6. What was *not* a phrase that Machen used to describe modernism?
   a. Collectivist age
   b. Mechanistic age
   c. Metallic age
   d. Spiritual age

Answer Key—Machen & Apologetics

REFLECTION & DISCUSSION QUESTIONS

Before the Video

What Do You Think?

These are personal questions. The answers should be based on your own knowledge and experience.

Scripture Reading

- In what context does Peter especially call us to be prepared to defend our faith?

  Peter calls us to be prepared to defend our faith in the context of suffering for it. When we suffer for the sake of the righteousness that is in keeping with our faith in the suffering Savior, we are to count ourselves blessed, just as Jesus taught us in the Sermon on the Mount (see Matt. 5:10–11). When we display this mentality and hope, we need to be prepared to give an answer for our hope, because it is in these moments of hope amid persecution that we look most strange to the world.

During the Video

Apologetics and Machen's Approach

- What is the meaning of the Greek words that make up the English word *apologetics*?

  Apologetics is from two Greek words. One of these words may be familiar to you, since it is related to the Apostle John's name for Christ in John 1:1: the Logos. *This word is related to the Greek verb* legō, *which means "to speak."* Apo *is a Greek preposition that means "to" or "toward," so* apologetics *is literally "to speak to" something. In Greek legal and philosophical contexts,* apologia *came to be a technical term, meaning "a reasoned defense."*

- What is often the context for the word *apologia* in the New Testament? What is the apologetic message of the New Testament?

  The word apologia *occurs eighteen times in the New Testament, and it often occurs in the context of a trial. Ten of these eighteen times occur in the books of Luke and Acts in the trial scenes of Jesus and the Apostles, and these scenes, especially in Acts, often involve a presentation of the gospel. Apologetics is essential to the very nature of the New Testament itself, because the New Testament is an apologetic for who Jesus is as the God-man and His work of redemption. It's an apologetic for the gospel.*

- In step with a classical approach to apologetics, where does Machen begin his apologetic arguments for the Christian faith?

It may be surprising to learn that Machen, who vigorously defended the inspiration and authority of Scripture, did not make the Bible the foundation of his approach to apologetics. Rather, Machen believed that apologetics should start with arguments for the existence of God and scientific treatments about the New Testament as a valid source of historical information.

Apologetics for the Church, Culture, and You

- How were liberal theologians distorting the gospel in the church? What was one of Machen's responses to this type of distortion?

  Liberals were denying the historicity of key events that are at the heart of the gospel. For instance, it was asserted that the resurrection did not need to be a historical event for it to have personal significance. One of Machen's responses to this type of distortion to the Christian faith was to defend the historicity of the virgin birth.

- What did Machen believe that modernism was creating in human life and culture?

  Machen believed that modernism was creating "an unparalleled impoverishment" of human life. Modernism, for all its technological advances, still could not address the problems that are faced by our souls, and it numbed people to the problem of sin such that they began to ignore the spiritual condition of their souls.

- In what sense is apologetics for the Christian?

  Apologetics is the reasoned defense of the Christian faith, so it involves answering naysayers, but it also affects our own understanding of the faith. Apologetics is necessary because we too can face doubts and discouragement. Machen believed, in this regard, that apologetics can make Christians "confident and joyous" when confronted with the doubts of an age of unbelief.

After the Video

- How does the New Testament call Christians to the task of apologetics?

  In many ways, the New Testament calls us to engage in the defense of the faith. One way it does this is through direct Apostolic command. The Apostle Peter calls us "to make a defense to anyone who asks you for a reason for the hope that is in you" (1 Peter 3:15). The New Testament is also filled with examples of people's defending the faith, such as Jesus and the Apostles' giving an apologia *in trial contexts in the books of Luke and Acts. Along these same lines, the Apostle Paul is imprisoned for his "defense [*apologia*] and confirmation of the gospel" (Phil. 1:7). The New Testament itself can be understood as an apologetic of the gospel, and insofar as Christians are called to share the gospel, they are called to engage in apologetics.*

- What is the order of Machen's apologetics?

  Machen believed that apologetics needs to start with arguments for the existence of God and scientific treatment for the New Testament documents that bear witness to the gospel. For Machen, apologetics presents the general truth about God and the Bible as a historical book, then the claims about the supernatural origin of the revelation in the Bible, and then the full truthfulness of the Bible as the Word of God. If someone sees that the Bible is trustworthy and sees that it claims to be the Word of God, then the Bible can be embraced as the Word of God.

- Why did Machen believe it was important to write a scholarly work on the virgin birth of Jesus Christ?

  In response to the denial of the historicity of Christianity that characterized liberalism, Machen wrote The Virgin Birth of Christ *in 1931. He believed that defending the virgin birth is itself a defense of the historicity of every other event in the Gospels. In this sense, the virgin birth of Christ can be understood as the first domino in an attack on the historic nature of Christianity. When the virgin birth is denied, error follows concerning who Jesus is as the God-man and the nature of His work on the cross.*

REVIEW QUIZ

1. **C.**
   Paul, in his letter to the Philippians, wrote that he was in prison for his defense, or apologia, *of the gospel. In this example, the word* apologia *is used in a theological context in the New Testament, whereas the other examples are set within a trial context.*

2. **A.**
   Machen embraced a classical approach to apologetics. He believed it was important to argue for the existence of God and to demonstrate that the Bible is the Word of God before having someone assume that it is the Word of God.

3. **C.**
   For Machen, embracing the Bible as the Word of God is the end of apologetics. His approach to apologetics involved, first, demonstrating that the Bible is historically trustworthy, and then showing where the Bible claims to be a book of divine origin, both of which taken together allow one to see the authority of the Bible as the Word of God.

4. **A.**
   The virgin birth was described as the first domino of liberal attacks on the historicity of the Gospels and the life, death, and resurrection of Jesus Christ. If someone denies the virgin birth, which is a denial of Jesus' person, then the significance of Jesus' work on the cross will be missed.

5. **C.**
   While each of these passages connects to the resurrection of Jesus Christ and rests on the historicity of the resurrection, Dr. Nichols referenced Paul's teaching in 1 Corinthians 15. Liberal theologians believed it was possible to deny the historicity of the resurrection yet still claim the resurrection of Jesus in one's heart, but Paul says, "If Christ has not been raised, . . . your faith is in vain" (v. 14).

6. **D.**
   Machen did not refer to modernism as "the spiritual age." Rather, Machen saw modernism with all its advances as something that distracted people from their spiritual problems.

6

Machen's Book

INTRODUCTION

J. Gresham Machen's classic *Christianity and Liberalism* is around one hundred years old, and it is still proving to be relevant and necessary. This is because its main subject matter is Christian truth, which never changes yet always seems to be under attack. In this lesson, Dr. Nichols provides the historical context of Machen's book to underscore why it was and is so urgently needed.

LEARNING GOALS

When you have finished this lesson, you should be able to:

- Explain why Machen titled his book *Christianity and Liberalism*
- Provide details about the historical context of the release of Machen's book
- Understand modernism in contrast with the fundamentals of the Christian faith

KEY IDEAS

- *Christianity and Liberalism* was a direct answer to Harry Emerson Fosdick's sermon "Shall the Fundamentalists Win?"
- Liberal theologians desired to accommodate Christianity to modernist sensibilities, and orthodox teachings about such things as creation, anthropology, and Scripture were abandoned.
- The early twentieth century can be equated to the period before the Reformation because the traditions of men were supplanting the Word of God.

REFLECTION & DISCUSSION QUESTIONS

Before the Video

What Do You Think?

Take a moment to answer the following questions. They will prepare you for the lecture.

- What are some nonnegotiable doctrines of the Christian faith?
- Why is the authority of the Bible crucial to disputes about doctrine? What happens when someone abandons the authority of Scripture?

Scripture Reading

All Scripture is breathed out by God and profitable for teaching, for reproof, for correction, and for training in righteousness, that the man of God may be complete, equipped for every good work.

—2 Timothy 3:16–17

- What phrase indicates the basis of Scripture's authority? How might this basis shape the way that we approach Scripture?

During the Video

Answer the following questions while you watch the video. They will guide you through the lecture.

The Rise of Modernism and Theological Liberalism *0:00–12:06*

- What is the thesis of *Christianity and Liberalism*?
- How was humanity viewed within modernism?
- In addition to modernist optimism, what other factors were contributing to attacks against fundamental Christian doctrine?

The Five Fundamentals and Machen's Response *12:06–24:41*

- What are the five fundamentals of the faith?

- What did Machen believe to be the answer to modernism?

After the Video

Answer the following questions after you have finished the lecture. They will help you identify and summarize the major points.

- How did the modernist perspective on human nature influence various Christian doctrines that are particularly important to the gospel?

  If you are in a group, have the members discuss how one's understanding of humanity influences one's understanding of the doctrines of grace, as summarized in the acrostic TULIP.

- How did Harry Emerson Fosdick explain away the inerrancy of Scripture, the virgin birth of Christ, and substitutionary atonement?

  If you are in a group, have the members discuss why it is inconsistent to esteem Jesus as merely a great moral teacher and example.

- How is it possible to compare the theological liberalism of the early twentieth century to the Roman Catholic Church before the Reformation?

  If you are in a group, have the members discuss how the Reformers provide us with an excellent example of how to handle the pressures of society for Christians to conform their beliefs to the culture or be silent about them altogether. Ask: Like the Reformers, where do we turn?

PRAYER

Commit what you have learned from God's Word in this lesson to prayer.

- Praise God for His authoritative Word in Scripture and for His Son, the Word made flesh, Jesus Christ.
- Confess any insecurities you might wrestle with that tempt you to accommodate your faith.
- Thank God that the truth of the gospel has lasting significance that does not need to change with the shifting sands of time.
- Ask God to give you deeper conviction of the truth so as to stand up for it when called on to do so and to share it with passion.

REVIEW QUIZ

Use these multiple-choice questions to measure what you learned from this lesson.

1. How did Harry Emerson Fosdick's teaching become popularized?
   a. His teaching was proliferated at the seminary level
   b. His teaching was received with enthusiasm because of its familiarity
   c. His teaching was broadcast and printed, being backed by John D. Rockefeller
   d. His teaching was controversial and garnered attention

2. What is *not* an element of modernism that influenced theological liberalism?
   a. Comparative religion
   b. Darwinian evolutionary theory
   c. Development of nuclear weapons
   d. Optimism of human progress

3. Who wrote in *Outlines of History* that humanity had entered a new stage of history that no longer required God?
   a. Harry Emerson Fosdick
   b. H.G. Wells
   c. John D. Rockefeller
   d. Pearl S. Buck

4. What word is central to Dr. Nichols' definition of liberalism?
   a. Tradition
   b. Separation
   c. Innovation
   d. Accommodation

5. The church as influenced by liberal theology is not comparable to the Roman Catholic Church before the Reformation because it was Protestant and stood on the authority of the Bible.
   a. True
   b. False

6. To whom did the word *fundamentalist* initially refer to?
   a. Christians who rejected scientific theory
   b. Christians who were politically conservative
   c. Christians who were willing to defend the fundamentals of the faith
   d. Christians who believed the fundamentals of the faith

Answer Key—Machen's Book

REFLECTION & DISCUSSION QUESTIONS

Before the Video

What Do You Think?

These are personal questions. The answers should be based on your own knowledge and experience.

Scripture Reading

- What phrase indicates the basis of Scripture's authority? How might this basis shape the way that we approach Scripture?

  In a rather poetic phrase, Paul tells us that all Scripture "is breathed out by God." God is over all, and as the source of Scripture, He gives it supreme authority over matters of faith and godliness. Because we are assured that God is the foundational authority undergirding the Bible's authority, we can trust Him in approaching the Bible, confident that it will accomplish the many purposes that we read of in this passage.

During the Video

The Rise of Modernism and Theological Liberalism

- What is the thesis of Christianity and Liberalism?

  The thesis of Christianity and Liberalism, *in a way, is contained in the title. There are two things: Christianity* and *liberalism. These two things are not the same. Machen's thesis is that liberalism is not Christianity. It's an entirely different thing that is outside the boundaries of the orthodox Christian faith.*

- How was humanity viewed within modernism?

  Prominent in the early twentieth century, modernism was the belief in human progress that was predicated on the idea that humanity is fundamentally good. In this understanding, societal structures are the source of the evil in the world. This viewpoint was underscored by the incredible advancements that were being achieved from 1880 to 1920, giving people a profound sense of optimism for the future.

- In addition to modernist optimism, what other factors were contributing to attacks against fundamental Christian doctrine?

  Even within the field of biblical scholarship there was a denigration of the Word of

God in the late nineteenth and early twentieth centuries. Accompanying this was the rise of comparative religious studies, other religions' being treated as equally valid with Christianity. Furthermore, Darwinian evolutionary theory was becoming popular as the preferred view of human origins.

The Five Fundamentals and Machen's Response

- What are the five fundamentals of the faith?

  The five fundamentals of the faith, which serve as the bedrock of fundamentalism, are the inerrancy of Scripture, the virgin birth of Christ, the penal substitutionary atonement of Christ, the bodily resurrection and return of Christ, and the historical reality of the miracles of Christ.

- What did Machen believe to be the answer to modernism?

  Writing Christianity and Liberalism *as a response to Fosdick and liberal theology as a whole, Machen believed that the answer to modernism was not the compromise for the sake of accommodation that so characterized the teaching of Fosdick. For Machen, the answer to modernism was the steadfast proclamation of the gospel of Jesus Christ.*

After the Video

- How did the modernist perspective on human nature influence various Christian doctrines that are particularly important to the gospel?

  From a modernist perspective, human beings are basically good. An outcome of holding such a view is that features of the gospel are entirely abandoned. When someone sees the problem of sin for what it truly is, the solution to that problem will be understood in a different light than if the problem is denied. The influence of modernism in theological circles led to the disavowal of truths such as God's holy wrath against sin, which has implications for how one views the atonement. Christ was thought to be no longer needed for the forgiveness of our sins.

- How did Harry Emerson Fosdick explain away the inerrancy of Scripture, the virgin birth of Christ, and substitutionary atonement?

  Fosdick explained away or reinterpreted many doctrines of the Christian faith. He did not believe that holding to the inerrancy of the Bible was necessary, falsely asserting that the doctrine of inerrancy is a new doctrine in church history that was not believed until its advancement by the Princetonians. Regarding the virgin birth and in line with comparative religious studies, he appealed to all the myths and legends in various other religions to dismiss the supernatural elements of Christianity as unbelievable. As for substitutionary atonement, he maintained that Jesus had not died in our place but died as an example.

- How is it possible to compare the theological liberalism of the early twentieth century to the Roman Catholic Church before the Reformation?

It is possible because both these traditions were emphasizing tradition over Scripture. The Roman Catholic Church placed its traditions on equal footing with the Bible in terms of authority, and as a result, the gospel was obscured. The liberal theology of the early twentieth century, in accommodating to modernism, also held the traditions and teaching of men in such high estimation that the church was losing sight of the gospel once again.

REVIEW QUIZ

1. **C.**
   Harry Emerson Fosdick had many platforms, but he also had the support of the wealthiest family in America, the Rockefellers. John D. Rockefeller made sure that Fosdick's teaching was broadcast over the airwaves, and he printed and distributed copies of Fosdick's sermon "Shall the Fundamentalists Win?" throughout the country by the tens of thousands.

2. **C.**
   Alongside the influences of comparative religious studies and the rising prevalence of Darwinian evolutionary theory, progress was giving people a profound sense of optimism about humanity and the human condition. This optimism would be stunted by the horrors of modern warfare, which is not a factor contributing to the emphases of liberal theology.

3. **B.**
   Apart from Rockefeller, Machen engaged with and challenged the ideas of Buck, Fosdick, and Wells. Wells wrote Outlines of History *and audaciously asserted that humanity had developed beyond God.*

4. **D.**
   While liberalism was certainly innovative, Dr. Nichols defined liberalism as "the accommodation of Christianity to modernist sensibilities." It is in this area of accommodation that the gospel is lost.

5. **B.**
   While the authority of Scripture and the purity of the gospel were at the heart of the Protestant Reformation, even Protestant churches can veer from the truth. In the early twentieth century, the church was questioning the authority of Scripture, the fundamental issue of the Reformation. For this reason, even though the controversy between liberalism and fundamentalism was a Protestant ordeal, the state of the church is comparable to that of the Roman Catholic Church before the Reformation.

6. **C.**
   While the word fundamentalist *has had negative connotations in recent history, the word was initially used in reference to what were known as the five fundamentals of the Christian faith. A fundamentalist was someone who not only believed these fundamentals but also was willing to contend for these fundamentals as convictions.*

7

Doctrine

INTRODUCTION

As a Christian, are you concerned with doctrine, or is Christianity something that should just be lived out? The liberal theologians of J. Gresham Machen's day denied the fundamental doctrinal content of the Christian faith and denied the very need for doctrine. In this lesson, Dr. Nichols launches into a guided tour through the chapters and doctrines of *Christianity and Liberalism*, which begins with a call to recognize the weight that the Bible places on correct doctrine.

LEARNING GOALS

When you have finished this lesson, you should be able to:

- Appreciate the ability of *Christianity and Liberalism* to speak to what Christians and the church are facing today
- Summarize the position of liberal theologians concerning the nature of the Christian faith and their approach to doctrine
- Trace Machen's argument for Christianity's being a doctrinal faith

KEY IDEAS

- Liberal theologians presented a version of Christianity that is not concerned with doctrine and is not itself a system of beliefs.
- Machen corrected the modern disbelief in doctrine itself by appealing to Paul's emphasis on doctrine and connecting it to Christ's own emphasis on doctrine, highlighting three texts of Scripture from Paul's letters and the Gospels, respectively.
- Paul taught the objective truth of the gospel message, the substance of which is the person of Jesus Christ and the objective truth of His own teaching and message.

REFLECTION & DISCUSSION QUESTIONS

Before the Video

What Do You Think?

Take a moment to answer the following questions. They will prepare you for the lecture.

- How did you come to a saving understanding of Jesus Christ? Was doctrine in any way involved?
- Can you live the Christian life faithfully apart from believing certain things? Why or why not?

Scripture Reading

Now I would remind you, brothers, of the gospel I preached to you, which you received, in which you stand, and by which you are being saved, if you hold fast to the word I preached to you—unless you believed in vain. For I delivered to you as of first importance what I also received: that Christ died for our sins in accordance with the Scriptures, that he was buried, [and] that he was raised on the third day in accordance with the Scriptures.

—1 Corinthians 15:1–4

- How does this passage underscore the importance of doctrine?

During the Video

Answer the following questions while you watch the video. They will guide you through the lecture.

Liberal Beliefs about Doctrine *0:00–9:11*

- What is the first way that liberal theologians redefined the Christian faith as it relates to doctrine?
- What is the second way that liberal theologians redefined the Christian faith as it relates to doctrine?

Paul's Beliefs about Doctrine *9:11–18:24*

- How does Dr. Nichols describe how the faith was transferred, beginning with Christ, from one person or group to another?

- How does Paul's stern declaration in Galatians 1 underscore the principle that sound doctrine is nonnegotiable in the Christian faith?

Christ's Beliefs about Doctrine *18:24–24:16*

- What is the "messianic mission"? How does it support the validity of doctrine?

- What statement, which follows the Sermon on the Mount, does away with the idea that Christianity is a lifestyle?

After the Video

Answer the following questions after you have finished the lecture. They will help you identify and summarize the major points.

- Paul was called to faithfully deliver what he had received. How do you know that you must also be faithful to learn and share sound doctrine?

  If you are in a group, have the members brainstorm about some devotional practices that promote consistent study and consideration of sound Christian doctrine.

- How does Paul's teaching in his last letter to Timothy particularly connect doctrine and life?

  If you are in a group, have the members critically consider what sort of Christian life would be left without doctrine. Ask: What would such a life look like? Are there any religious practices in your life that are unrelated to doctrine?

- How did Jesus comfort His anxious disciples in the upper room? What word can summarize the would-be source of the disciples' comfort? How does this source provide you comfort in your own anxieties?

  If you are in a group, have the members scan John 14–17 for the prominent word that Dr. Nichols mentioned, and have them read the passages in which it appears.

PRAYER

Commit what you have learned from God's Word in this lesson to prayer.

- Praise God for being the God of truth, whose Word is truth (John 17:17).
- Confess any tendencies you have to avoid studying the doctrines of the faith.
- Thank God for the clear teachings of Scripture concerning salvation.
- Ask God to bless your study of His Word with the truth of the Spirit.

REVIEW QUIZ

Use these multiple-choice questions to measure what you learned from this lesson.

1. Reformation doctrines such as *sola Scriptura* and *sola fide* would be considered core to Christian experience by the liberal faction of Machen's day.
   a. True
   b. False
2. Why did Machen need to appeal to both Paul's and Jesus' teachings about doctrine?
   a. Paul is difficult to understand.
   b. Jesus taught about doctrine only indirectly.
   c. Paul was suspect among liberal theologians.
   d. Jesus balances Paul's teaching about doctrine.
3. From whom did Paul receive the gospel?
   a. James
   b. Jesus
   c. John
   d. Peter
4. Hypothetically speaking, Paul would have been sympathetic to the liberal teachings of Machen's day, though he would have corrected them.
   a. True
   b. False
5. Which of the following was *not* a passage that Machen used to defend doctrine from Paul's letters?
   a. 1 Corinthians 15
   b. Galatians 1
   c. Colossians 1
   d. 2 Timothy 2

6. Which of the following was *not* a passage that Machen used to defend doctrine from the Gospels?
   a. The messianic mission statement of Mark
   b. The parable of the faithful servant
   c. The Sermon on the Mount
   d. The Upper Room Discourse

Answer Key—Doctrine

REFLECTION & DISCUSSION QUESTIONS

Before the Video

What Do You Think?

These are personal questions. The answers should be based on your own knowledge and experience.

Scripture Reading

- How does this passage underscore the importance of doctrine?

  Paul writes about the gospel as a teaching that is "received." The Corinthians "received" from Paul what he himself "received" as an Apostle of Jesus Christ. He calls them to "hold fast" to this word, which outlines essential facts about the life, death, burial, and resurrection of Jesus Christ, all of which were "in accordance with the Scriptures." Christianity is a doctrinal faith.

During the Video

Liberal Beliefs about Doctrine

- What is the first way that liberal theologians redefined the Christian faith as it relates to doctrine?

  First, liberal theologians recast Christianity not as a belief system that is made up of essential doctrines but as a life. Christianity, understood in this way, is about behaviors and not beliefs.

- What is the second way that liberal theologians redefined the Christian faith as it relates to doctrine?

  Second, liberal theologians interpreted doctrine as something foreign to the heart of Christian experience. Doctrines, therefore, have been articulated in different ways throughout church history and can change over time. Doctrine is not the unchanging "kernel" of Christian experience.

Paul's Beliefs about Doctrine

- How does Dr. Nichols describe how the faith was transferred, beginning with Christ, from one person or group to another?

  In 1 Corinthians 15:3, Paul writes, "For I delivered to you as of first importance what I also received." Paul received the message of the gospel from Christ Himself, just as the other Apostles did. Christ delivered His teachings to the Apostles, who, in turn, inscripturated His teachings and passed down those teachings in their training of church officers.

- How does Paul's stern declaration in Galatians 1 underscore the principle that sound doctrine is nonnegotiable in the Christian faith?

  In Galatians 1:9, Paul writes, "If anyone is preaching to you a gospel contrary to the one you received, let him be accursed." Previously, Paul proclaimed this same anathema on anyone, including the Apostles or even an angel from heaven, who preached a different gospel. The gospel is itself a message and not a lifestyle. It is something that can be taught falsely, and Paul's strong language is a rebuke against false teaching.

Christ's Beliefs about Doctrine

- What is the "messianic mission"? How does it support the validity of doctrine?

  The "messianic mission" is described in Mark 10:45, in which Jesus Himself tells us why He came: "to give his life as a ransom for many." Jesus came with the mission that was an event—His death on the cross—that has a meaning. The historic nature and significance of that event is a point of doctrine.

- What statement, which follows the Sermon on the Mount, does away with the idea that Christianity is a lifestyle?

  Liberal theologians often appealed to the Sermon on the Mount as the primary evidence that Christianity was a life and not fundamentally concerned with doctrine. The Sermon on the Mount ends, however, by underscoring the impact of Jesus' teaching: "And when Jesus finished these sayings, the crowds were astonished at his teaching, *for he was* teaching *them as one who had authority, and not as their scribes" (Matt. 7:28–29, emphasis added).*

After the Video

- Paul was called to faithfully deliver what he had received. How do you know that you must also be faithful to learn and share sound doctrine?

  Answers may vary, but consider how Paul received the gospel directly from Jesus Christ. Like the other Apostles, he inscripturated the teaching that he had received and raised up and trained elders and pastors, such as Timothy. As a member of a church, as a Christian, you ought to expect this same body of teaching to be handed down to you, and once it is delivered to you, you likewise have an obligation to faithfully guard and transmit it.

- How does Paul's teaching in his last letter to Timothy particularly connect doctrine and life?

  Machen appealed to Paul's instruction in 2 Timothy 2:2–3 to show how intimately doctrine is connected to the Christian life. Paul first appeals to Timothy to be strengthened based on the grace of Jesus Christ and what Paul had taught him—"what you have heard from me" (v. 2). Paul also charged Timothy to deliver this teaching over to others who could also teach. Connecting such teaching to the Christian life is Paul's following command: "Share in suffering as a good soldier of Christ" (v. 3). The doctrines of the faith are connected to the life of the faith.

- How did Jesus comfort His anxious disciples in the upper room? What word can summarize the would-be source of the disciples' comfort? How does this source provide you comfort in your own anxieties?

  In the upper room, the disciples were very anxious after hearing Jesus' announcement that He would soon be leaving them. To comfort His disciples, He promised them the Holy Spirit, another Comforter, who would lead them into the truth. The word truth *is prominent throughout Jesus' Upper Room Discourse, and it is profound to consider that when His disciples were most anxious, He comforted them with truth—doctrine.*

REVIEW QUIZ

1. **B.**
   While it may seem that one would recognize how foundational these doctrines are for the Christian faith, the liberal theologians of Machen's day dismissed such doctrines' being essential to the heart of Christian experience. They rather saw them as expressions of the faith from bygone eras, making doctrine something that could be changed or discarded entirely.

2. **C.**
   Liberal theologians favored Jesus over Paul, believing Paul to have distorted or added to the "true" faith of Jesus Christ. For this reason, Machen defended the legitimacy of doctrine at the heart of the Christian faith from passages of Scripture from both Paul and Jesus.

3. **B.**
   In 1 Corinthians 15:3, Paul writes, "For I delivered to you as of first importance what I also received." Some knowledge about Paul's conversion and the immediate years that followed it are important for understanding that Paul received the gospel initially and directly from Christ. He only confirmed his understanding of the gospel later with the Apostles (see Gal. 1:11–2:10).

4. **B.**
   One gets the impression from Paul's teaching that though he was pastorally sensitive to the needs of Christians, he would not have tolerated the distortions of the liberal theologians. The gospel was at stake, and Paul connected doctrine to the Christian life so closely that he would not have had a category for understanding the liberal claim that Christianity is merely a lifestyle.

5. **C.**
   Though it can also be understood as a call to stand firm for Jesus Christ, not being held captive to human traditions but resting in the fullness of Christ, Colossians 1

was not a passage that Machen used to defend the legitimacy of doctrine in Christianity and Liberalism.

6. **B.**
   In many ways, the parable of the faithful servant can be used as a severe warning to the liberal theologians of Machen's day, for they were not being faithful to the gospel with which we have been entrusted. This passage, however, was not one of the places that Machen referenced to defend the legitimacy of doctrine from the teachings of Jesus.

8

God & Man

INTRODUCTION

The study of doctrine is the study of theology, which is itself the study of God. If we are to ever understand ourselves, then we need to understand God, knowing who He is and what He demands of us. In this lesson, Dr. Nichols continues into the next chapter of J. Gresham Machen's classic work, presenting how Machen approaches liberal distortions about both the nature of God and the nature of man.

LEARNING GOALS

When you have finished this lesson, you should be able to:

- Distinguish between liberal and biblical views of God and man
- Explain how understanding God connects to our own self-understanding

KEY IDEAS

- The answer to the question "Who is God?" has everything to do with answering the question "Who are we?" The two questions go together and reference one another.
- God is knowable—not only through His special revelation in Scripture but also through His general revelation in creation and our awareness of His moral law.
- A flawed understanding of God and a flawed understanding of who we are obscure the glory of the gospel.

REFLECTION & DISCUSSION QUESTIONS

Before the Video

What Do You Think?

Take a moment to answer the following questions. They will prepare you for the lecture.

- Why are spiritual experiences alone insufficient for understanding God?

- Considering who God is and who we are, why did the Son of God become a man?

Scripture Reading

> *For the wrath of God is revealed from heaven against all ungodliness and unrighteousness of men, who by their unrighteousness suppress the truth. For what can be known about God is plain to them, because God has shown it to them. For his invisible attributes, namely, his eternal power and divine nature, have been clearly perceived, ever since the creation of the world, in the things that have been made. So they are without excuse. For although they knew God, they did not honor him as God or give thanks to him, but they became futile in their thinking, and their foolish hearts were darkened.*
>
> —Romans 1:18–21

- What does the suppression of the knowledge of God result in?

During the Video

Answer the following questions while you watch the video. They will guide you through the lecture.

The Knowable God — *0:00–8:55*

- How does nature teach us about God's existence?

- What does every person's sense of justice teach us about our relationship with God?

The Liberal Doctrine of God — *8:55–19:24*

- Is God knowable, according to liberal theologians?

- What is the universal fatherhood of God? Is this teaching wrong in every sense?

- What did liberal theologians teach about God's transcendence and immanence?

The Liberal Doctrine of Man *19:24–24:24*

- What do people lose a sense of under the liberal teachings about God?

- What did Machen fault about the preachers so prominent in his day?

After the Video

Answer the following questions after you have finished the lecture. They will help you identify and summarize the major points.

- In what ways do the three liberal teachings about God in this lecture connect to one another? Do they contradict themselves in any way?

  If you are in a group, have the members discuss what Machen meant by calling God's immanence His "bright side." Ask: In what ways can you also see God's transcendence as a "bright side"?

- What are orthodox views of the doctrine of God in response to the three liberal teachings about God in this lecture?

  If you are in a group, have the members discuss how these orthodox teachings about God connect to one another.

- Why ought Christians to be humble in their own identity as children of God and as they sit under the preached Word of God?

  If you are in a group, have the members discuss how pride can be contradictory to such things as worship, evangelism, and mercy ministry.

PRAYER

Commit what you have learned from God's Word in this lesson to prayer.

- Praise God for His mighty transcendence above creation.
- Confess areas of pridefulness that obscure the beauty of God's grace.
- Thank God for making Himself known in Christ and being truly immanent to us through the indwelling Holy Spirit.
- Ask God to help you to remain humble yet joyfully secure in your identity as a child of God.

REVIEW QUIZ

Use these multiple-choice questions to measure what you learned from this lesson.

1. It is absolutely impious to speak of God as awful.
    a. True
    b. False
2. What key phrase does Machen use to define the knowability of God through theistic proofs?
    a. General revelation
    b. Special revelation
    c. Rational theism
    d. Experiential theism
3. Which attribute of God most closely relates to His immanence?
    a. Aseity
    b. Eternality
    c. Holiness
    d. Omnipresence
4. Who said that God is both *Deus absconditus* and *Deus revelatus*?
    a. Augustine
    b. John Calvin
    c. Jonathan Edwards
    d. Martin Luther
5. Only imagining God as transcendent can lessen someone's sense of burden over his or her sins.
    a. True
    b. False
6. What key term summarizes what Machen considered to be an important posture for our reception of God's grace?
    a. Fear
    b. Gratitude
    c. Humility
    d. Servitude

Answer Key—God & Man

REFLECTION & DISCUSSION QUESTIONS

Before the Video

What Do You Think?

These are personal questions. The answers should be based on your own knowledge and experience.

Scripture Reading

- What does the suppression of the knowledge of God result in?

  This passage plainly reveals that all people know something about God's existence and attributes. The suppression of this knowledge first results in a person's dishonoring God and not giving Him the appropriate gratitude, which in turn results in a futile mind and darkened heart. Because God is worthy of all honor, worship, and thanksgiving, He is justly displeased.

During the Video

The Knowable God

- How does nature teach us about God's existence?

  Dr. Nichols provided numerous philosophical explanations for how nature teaches us about God's existence. The fact that in creation there is something rather than nothing points back to God as Creator, and many theistic proofs for God's existence are based on looking at the effects found in nature as argument for God's existence.

- What does every person's sense of justice teach us about our relationship with God?

  Each and every person, by virtue of being made in the image of God, has a sense of justice that indicates an inherent awareness of God's moral law. We understand that God Himself is just, such that we ultimately understand that we are accountable to Him.

The Liberal Doctrine of God

- Is God knowable, according to liberal theologians?

  Liberal theologians did not emphasize the knowability of God, which would affirm the validity of doctrine. Rather, they denied that God was knowable and stressed our felt experience of God, which is in line with their teaching that Christianity is a life.

- What is the universal fatherhood of God? Is this teaching wrong in every sense?

  The universal fatherhood of God is the belief that everyone is a child of God. This teaching goes beyond the acknowledgment that everyone is created by God, which is the only appropriate sense in which it can be affirmed. In its fullest sense, being a child of God involves a salvific relationship to the Father through Jesus Christ.

- What did liberal theologians teach about God's transcendence and immanence?

  Liberal theologians stressed God's immanence to the neglect of teaching His transcendence, which would involve teaching on such attributes as God's holiness. They believed that God is fully immanent, which is not who God truly is.

The Liberal Doctrine of Man

- What do people lose a sense of under the liberal teachings about God?

  When people fall under such beliefs that our felt experience of God is what matters most, that we are all children of God, and that God is fully immanent to us, we lose sight of the gulf between us as creatures and God as our transcendent Creator. And when we lose sight of this gulf, we lose sight of our sin, leading us to pridefulness.

- What did Machen fault about the preachers so prominent in his day?

  Machen ended his chapter "God and Man" by faulting the preachers of his day for not preaching repentance, which would call people to relinquish their pride and humbly receive the grace of God. Instead, liberal preachers would present the faith as if it were good enough for the people.

After the Video

- In what ways do the three liberal teachings about God in this lecture connect to one another? Do they contradict themselves in any way?

  Answers to this question may vary. Consider how liberalism teaches that our relationship to God is primarily through felt experience, and this intimately connects to the idea that God is fully immanent, that He is near to us. If God is fully immanent, then He also has a closeness with His creatures akin to the relationship between a father and his children. There does seem to be a contradiction, however, in the relationship between a felt experience of God and His immanence. Liberalism pits felt experience against the importance of having knowledge of God, but this seems to contradict the idea that God is immanent. As Deus revelatus, *He is immanent in making Himself known.*

- What are orthodox views of the doctrine of God in response to the three liberal teachings about God in this lecture?

  Concerning God's knowability, orthodox Christianity affirms that God has revealed His existence and attributes in creation and in the consciences of His creatures, and He has also revealed Himself salvifically in Scripture and especially in Jesus Christ. Concerning God's fatherhood, orthodox Christianity affirms that God is truly a Father to all those who trust in Jesus Christ. Concerning God's nature, orthodox Christianity affirms not only that He is immanent but also that He is transcendent.

- Why ought Christians to be humble in their own identity as children of God and as they sit under the preached Word of God?

  While the liberal teaching of the universal fatherhood of God is false, it would be wrong for Christians to pride themselves on being children of God as if they were in an exclusive club. Our being elect children of God is through the grace of Jesus Christ. Likewise, when we sit under the preached Word of God, being humble allows us to see the true weight of our sin before a holy God, and when we are able to recognize this, we can behold the glory of God's grace in Jesus Christ.

REVIEW QUIZ

1. **B.**
   While modern usage of the word awful *has negative connotations, the word was once understood as an adjective describing something that inspires awe, something that is fearful in its majesty. Machen, therefore, used this word in reference to God.*

2. **C.**
   General revelation and special revelation are both connected to God's knowability, for these are the means through which He has revealed Himself. Machen used the phrase rational theism, *in particular, to articulate God's knowability through theistic proofs made possible by God's revelation.*

3. **D.**
   God is omnipresent, meaning He is everywhere. This attribute of God most closely connects to His immanence, that He is a God near to His people. The other attributes connect most to His exalted and majestic transcendence.

4. **D.**
   Luther said that God is both Deus absconditus *and* Deus revelatus, *the "hidden God" and the "revealed God." God is both transcendent and immanent. He is unknown and known.*

5. **B.**
   Liberalism magnifies God's immanence to avoid wrestling with the accountability that we have before God as our transcendent Lord. When we lose sight of God's transcendence, we might feel less of a burden for our sin yet also lose any sense of our need for a Savior.

6. **C.**
The problem with the liberal doctrine of man is that it can make us secure in our sin as we ignore it and we pridefully see ourselves as fundamentally good people. When there's pride in the human heart, then there will be no room for the grace of God, which is why we need humility.

9

The Bible

INTRODUCTION

After establishing the validity of doctrine and the importance of knowing who God is so that we can know who we are, J. Gresham Machen moves to defend the Bible against the modernist tendencies of liberal theologians. This is essential because Christianity is a message, and that message is contained in the Bible. In this lesson, Dr. Nichols stresses the relevance of defending the authority of Scripture in our own day and examines Machen's ever-applicable answers as to why the Bible is our certain source of truth.

LEARNING GOALS

When you have finished this lesson, you should be able to:

- Summarize three modern-day challenges to the authority of Scripture
- Describe three key doctrines that define the nature of Scripture

KEY IDEAS

- The Bible is the inspired and inerrant revealed Word of God and is therefore true.
- The cultural Christianity that characterized the liberalism of Machen's day still exists.
- The doctrines of the revelation, inspiration, and inerrancy undergird our confidence in the Bible, which stands alone among every other religious text.

REFLECTION & DISCUSSION QUESTIONS

Before the Video

What Do You Think?

Take a moment to answer the following questions. They will prepare you for the lecture.

- What are the greatest threats to the authority of the Bible today?

- How do you know that the Bible is true?

Scripture Reading

I have manifested your name to the people whom you gave me out of the world. Yours they were, and you gave them to me, and they have kept your word. Now they know that everything that you have given me is from you. For I have given them the words that you gave me, and they have received them and have come to know in truth that I came from you; and they have believed that you sent me. . . . But now I am coming to you, and these things I speak in the world, that they may have my joy fulfilled in themselves. I have given them your word, and the world has hated them because they are not of the world, just as I am not of the world. I do not ask that you take them out of the world, but that you keep them from the evil one. They are not of the world, just as I am not of the world. Sanctify them in the truth; your word is truth.

—John 17:6–8, 13–17

- In light of this passage, why ought the Bible to have a central place in the Christian life?

During the Video

Answer the following questions while you watch the video. They will guide you through the lecture.

Present Challenges *0:00–10:52*

- What is the core assertion of postmodernism?

- Why is secularism so challenging to answer?

Timeless Answers *10:52–24:48*

- What is at the center of special revelation?

- What is verbal plenary inspiration?

- What two approaches does Machen take to deal with criticism over the Bible's authority and trustworthiness?

After the Video

Answer the following questions after you have finished the lecture. They will help you identify and summarize the major points.

- Which of the three modern problems that were introduced by Dr. Nichols do you consider to be the greatest challenge to Christianity and why?

  If you are in a group, have the members discuss their answers to the question above. Ask: Which of these three have you most struggled with personally or have you encountered in conversations about the faith with others?

- Why are the doctrines of inspiration and inerrancy so closely connected? What is the problematic implication of the liberal theologian's affirmation that the Bible is inspired but not inerrant?

  If you are in a group, have the members discuss why inerrancy is a central doctrine of evangelicalism. Ask: Is certainty about anything possible without this doctrine?

- How do Machen's two points about the external and internal evidence of the truth of the New Testament work together?

  If you are in a group, have the members discuss what external and internal evidence has been most compelling to them about the trustworthiness and the truthfulness of the Bible.

PRAYER

Commit what you have learned from God's Word in this lesson to prayer.

- Praise God for plainly declaring His will for our salvation in Scripture and sending His Son, the Word made flesh, to accomplish it.
- Confess any unwillingness you might face in sharing the truth of Scripture because of the attitudes of our society toward it.
- Thank God for making His Word alive to you in the full conviction of the Holy Spirit.
- Ask God to help you in your continued study of His Word.

REVIEW QUIZ

Use these multiple-choice questions to measure what you learned from this lesson.

1. What word most closely connects to the concept of truth in the view of postmodernism and pluralism?
   a. Objective
   b. Personal
   c. Absolute
   d. Timeless
2. Natural theology is possible because of general revelation.
   a. True
   b. False
3. What word is related to the Greek term used in John 1:18 about Jesus' work in making the Father known?
   a. Revelation
   b. Reason
   c. Illumination
   d. Exegesis
4. Special revelation is called "special" because it is for the elect of God.
   a. True
   b. False
5. Which of the following best describes the process of inspiration?
   a. The Holy Spirit's mechanical use of human authors to physically write Scripture through them
   b. The Holy Spirit's superintendence of human authors in the use of their own faculties and experiences to write the very words of Scripture
   c. The Holy Spirit's selecting gifted and morally superior authors who would not need supernatural aid to write Scripture
   d. The Holy Spirit's use of divinely chosen authors to write the general sense of what God wants to reveal in Scripture
6. Which New Testament author did Machen use to argue that these authors recognized that they were writing Scripture?
   a. James
   b. John
   c. Luke
   d. Peter

Answer Key—The Bible

REFLECTION & DISCUSSION QUESTIONS

Before the Video

What Do You Think?

These are personal questions. The answers should be based on your own knowledge and experience.

Scripture Reading

- In light of this passage, why ought the Bible to have a central place in the Christian life?

  Jesus taught the disciples the very words that were given to Him by the Father, and the Apostles, in turn, wrote down this teaching in Scripture. When we read the Bible, we are reading God's Word, and Jesus prayed that we would be sanctified through this Word. The Bible ought to have a central place in our lives because of its source and because it is the source through which the Holy Spirit most ordinarily works for our sanctification.

During the Video

Present Challenges

- What is the core assertion of postmodernism?

  Postmodernism fundamentally rejects truth. At its core, it is an assertion of hyper-relativism that sees the quest for truth as unnecessary, elusive, or impossible. While rejecting objective truth, it affirms the possibility of and prioritizes personal truths.

- Why is secularism so challenging to answer?

  To some degree, an atheist, who totally rejects God and His existence, is easier to engage in an apologetic discussion because at least the atheist has considered weighty questions about God in the first place. Secularism has introduced the idea that belief in God is merely one equal option among many, and for this reason, people are apathetic about God.

Timeless Answers

- What is at the center of special revelation?

  At the center of special revelation is the person Jesus Christ. He is Himself the Logos of God. He is the supreme revelation as the Word of God because, as the Son of God, He became flesh and revealed the Father to us (see John 1:18).

- What is verbal plenary inspiration?

  The doctrine of the Bible's inspiration asserts that God superintended by the Holy Spirit the writing of human authors, utilizing all their personalities and experiences in such a way that Scripture can be understood as both a divine and a human work. When speaking about verbal plenary inspiration, the word verbal *refers to the fact that the very words of Scripture (not just its concepts) are inspired, and the word* plenary *refers to the fact that all Scripture (not just some parts of it) is inspired.*

- What two approaches does Machen take to deal with criticism over the Bible's authority and trustworthiness?

  To answer the critics of the Bible, Machen appealed to external and internal evidence of Scripture's authority and trustworthiness. External manuscript evidence shows that the books of the New Testament were written early, so critical claims that these works were late and not reflective of the teaching of Christ and the Apostles are false. The Apostles' self-awareness as authors of Scripture is part of the internal evidence of the authority and trustworthiness of Scripture, which has an internal cohesion in giving us a picture of who Jesus is and what the church is to believe.

After the Video

- Which of the three modern problems that were introduced by Dr. Nichols do you consider to be the greatest challenge to Christianity and why?

  The answer to this question explores your own impression of whether postmodernism, pluralism, or secularism is the greatest challenge to faith and its advancement.

- Why are the doctrines of inspiration and inerrancy so closely connected? What is the problematic implication of the liberal theologian's affirmation that the Bible is inspired but not inerrant?

  It is a small step from the doctrine of inspiration to the doctrine of inerrancy. Since the Bible is the inspired Word of God, then it is, by definition, without error. The Bible is true because God is true. To say that the Bible does contain errors at various points is problematic because of this close connection between the doctrines of inspiration and inerrancy. If we were to say that the Bible is riddled with errors, we would question the character of God, who inspired it.

- How do Machen's two points about the external and internal evidence of the truth of the New Testament work together?

  Machen defended the Bible by pointing to external and internal witnesses to its veracity. The New Testament is based on eyewitness testimony, so when Machen appealed to the external manuscript evidence that the Gospels and the letters of the New Testament are early documents, he validated the eyewitness testimony within those documents because the New Testament was written in a period when those eyewitness testimonies could be objectively confirmed.

REVIEW QUIZ

1. **B.**
While truth can and should have personal significance, truth goes beyond each and every one of us. We do not construct truth in such a way as to claim our own personal truth. Yet this kind of thinking is typical of postmodernism and pluralism.

2. **A.**
Because God has revealed Himself in the things that have been made, it is possible to reason from these things for God's existence and substantiate some things about His character. God reveals Himself through nature in general revelation, and natural theology concerns theology that is known by nature.

3. **D.**
John 1:18 reads, "No one has ever seen God; the only God, who is at the Father's side, he has made him known." The verb in the last phrase that is translated "has made . . . known" is exegesatō. *This Greek word is related to a common English word that is used in biblical studies:* exegesis.

4. **B.**
The terms general revelation *and* special revelation *do communicate something about who receives these types of revelation. General revelation, for instance, is universal, so everyone receives God's general revelation. But that does not mean that God's special revelation in Scripture is for the elect only; many hear or read the Word of God yet reject it.*

5. **B.**
The Holy Spirit's mechanical dictation of Scripture through a human author is a common misconception of inspiration. The doctrine of inspiration affirms the Holy Spirit's superintendence of divine Scripture while at the same time affirming that Scripture is a human work. Yet this work isn't merely a human work; all Scripture is the Word of God, and every part of it is inspired down to its very words.

6. **D.**
Various arguments can be made about how the authors of the New Testament were aware that they were writing Scripture. One classic text from the Apostle Peter makes this case particularly apparent: "And count the patience of our Lord as salvation, just as our beloved brother Paul also wrote to you according to the wisdom given him, as he does in all his letters when he speaks in them of these matters. There are some things in them that are hard to understand, which the ignorant and unstable twist to their own destruction, as they do the other Scriptures*" (2 Peter 3:15–16, emphasis added).*

10

Christ

INTRODUCTION

Christianity and Liberalism is logically organized. After J. Gresham Machen addresses the subject of the Bible, he can now move on to the message of the Bible. The Bible contains the message of the gospel, and that message is essentially about a person—Jesus Christ. In this lesson, Dr. Nichols demonstrates how the distortions of liberalism concerning the person and work of Christ were a distortion of the gospel itself.

LEARNING GOALS

When you have finished this lesson, you should be able to:

- Differentiate the Christ of liberalism from the Christ of Christianity
- Explain in what sense it is appropriate and inappropriate to look to Jesus as an example
- Summarize Machen's arguments against the teachings of liberalism concerning the person and work of Christ

KEY IDEAS

- Christ is not merely a selfless example; He is a sinless substitute.
- The miracles that Jesus performed during His earthly ministry cannot be called into doubt without calling His identity into doubt.
- Biblical Christianity affirms fully that Jesus is both truly God and truly man.

REFLECTION & DISCUSSION QUESTIONS

Before the Video

What Do You Think?

Take a moment to answer the following questions. They will prepare you for the lecture.

- How do you follow Christ as an example? In what ways can we not imitate Christ?

- Is church discipline a mark of a faithful church? Why or why not?

Scripture Reading

For all who rely on works of the law are under a curse; for it is written, "Cursed be everyone who does not abide by all things written in the Book of the Law, and do them." Now it is evident that no one is justified before God by the law, for "The righteous shall live by faith." But the law is not of faith, rather "The one who does them shall live by them." Christ redeemed us from the curse of the law by becoming a curse for us—for it is written, "Cursed is everyone who is hanged on a tree."

—Galatians 3:10–13

- What, on the one hand, is comforting about this passage and what, on the other hand, can be terrifying about it?

During the Video

Answer the following questions while you watch the video. They will guide you through the lecture.

The Christ of Liberalism *0:00–9:40*

- What is liberalism's primary view of Jesus and His death? But why is Jesus different from us?

- What results in the Christian life from merely viewing Jesus in terms of imitation and not imputation?

The Christ of Christianity *9:40–24:26*

- Why does Machen focus on Jesus' miracles to argue against liberalism's conception of Christ?

- How does the New Testament affirm both Jesus' humanity and His divinity?

After the Video

Answer the following questions after you have finished the lecture. They will help you identify and summarize the major points.

- How does liberalism's understanding of the relationship of faith to Jesus Christ differ from orthodox Christianity's understanding?

  If you are in a group, have the members read Deuteronomy 21:22–23 to provide the Old Testament context of Galatians 3:10–13. Ask: How does the violation of the law and the defilement in this passage of Deuteronomy relate to the gospel?

- How do you practically pursue Christlikeness in your life? How does this pursuit relate to an active reflection on what Christ has objectively done for you in the gospel?

  If you are in a group, have the members discuss why it is important to see Jesus as both our Savior and our example. Ask: What is a potential problem of thinking about Jesus only in terms of imputation and not also in terms of imitation?

- How do rejecting substitutionary atonement, rejecting miracles, and rejecting the deity of Christ logically connect?

  If you are in a group, have the members read John 11. Ask: How does John 11 connect a right view of Jesus' death, miraculous signs, and divinity?

PRAYER

Commit what you have learned from God's Word in this lesson to prayer.

- Praise God for His holiness.
- Confess any sins that are particularly weighing on you.
- Thank God for sending His most holy Son, who imputes His righteousness to us.
- Ask God to help you imitate Christ in obedience to Scripture by the power of the Holy Spirit.

REVIEW QUIZ

Use these multiple-choice questions to measure what you learned from this lesson.

1. Who said that Jesus is the "fairest flower of humanity"?
   a. Charles Spurgeon
   b. Harry Emerson Fosdick
   c. J. Gresham Machen
   d. Martin Luther
2. What Old Testament passage is quoted in both Romans and Galatians?
   a. "Cursed is everyone who is hanged on a tree."
   b. "Cursed be everyone who does not abide by all things written in the Book of the Law, and do them."
   c. "In you shall all the nations be blessed."
   d. "The righteous shall live by faith."
3. What prepositional phrase from the Nicene Creed underscores a key doctrine from this lecture?
   a. "Unto us"
   b. "Through us"
   c. "For us"
   d. "About us"
4. Denying the reality of miracles is typical of the movement that aimed to distinguish the "Jesus of history" from the "Jesus of faith."
   a. True
   b. False
5. The doctrine of the divinity of Jesus Christ was developed in the early ecumenical creeds of the church.
   a. True
   b. False
6. What term summarizes the formula that Jesus has two natures in one person?
   a. Substantial union
   b. Spiritual union
   c. Material union
   d. Hypostatic union

Answer Key—Christ

REFLECTION & DISCUSSION QUESTIONS

Before the Video

What Do You Think?

These are personal questions. The answers should be based on your own knowledge and experience.

Scripture Reading

- What, on the one hand, is comforting about this passage and what, on the other hand, can be terrifying about it?

  It is profoundly comforting to reflect on the reality that Jesus Christ became a curse on behalf of His people through His death on the cross, yet it is profoundly terrifying to consider that apart from faith in Him, people perish under the curse of the law.

During the Video

The Christ of Liberalism

- What is liberalism's primary view of Jesus and His death? But why is Jesus different from us?

  The Christ of liberalism is merely an example, and His death is therefore seen as the supreme example of selflessness that Christians are to imitate. This, however, is not a complete picture of who Jesus is. He is not merely a selfless example, but He is a sinless substitute. He is unlike us in that He is spotless, pure, without sin, enabling Him to stand in the place of sinners like us.

- What results in the Christian life from merely viewing Jesus in terms of imitation and not imputation?

  Liberalism, with its emphasis on imitating Christ as an example without affirming imputation, creates a burden for the Christian to step up, pull it together, and go about the Christian life in his or her own strength. In this, the Christian strives for a righteousness that is his or her own, whereas the doctrine of imputation teaches us that Christ has given us His righteousness just as He has taken our sin.

The Christ of Christianity

- Why does Machen focus on Jesus' miracles to argue against liberalism's conception of Christ?

  Liberalism rejects the miracles of Jesus Christ from His virgin birth to His resurrection. The problem with this is that, in doing so, liberalism rejects who Jesus claimed to be. Machen focuses on the miracles of Jesus Christ to defend His identity because miracles function in the Bible to attest to who someone is. In the case of Moses, miracles pointed to the reality that he was God's appointed prophet. In the case of Jesus, miracles pointed to the reality that He is God's Son and the Savior.

- How does the New Testament affirm both Jesus' humanity and His divinity?

  Throughout the Gospels, we read about very ordinary and human moments of Jesus' life. Like us, He was born and developed in an ordinary way. Jesus became hungry, thirsty, and tired in the same way that we do. Yet unlike us, He also performed miracles, and He claimed to be the Son of God, equal with the Father. The "I am" statements in John's gospel particularly indicate Jesus' understanding of His deity.

After the Video

- How does liberalism's understanding of the relationship of faith to Jesus Christ differ from orthodox Christianity's understanding?

  Liberalism teaches that Jesus Christ is our example of faith. This is true, but when this truth is presented as the whole truth, it is misleading. Jesus, to be sure, believed and trusted in God, but not for His justification. Jesus kept the law perfectly and so was perfectly righteous. In this sense, Jesus ought to be our example, but He is not merely our example. Orthodox Christianity teaches that Jesus is the object of our faith and that to be justified, we must place our faith in Him.

- How do you practically pursue Christlikeness in your life? How does this pursuit relate to an active reflection on what Christ has objectively done for you in the gospel?

  The answers to these questions are personal and may vary but should consider what the reality of imputation—that Christ has taken your sin and has given you His righteousness—provides you in your pursuit of holiness.

- How do rejecting substitutionary atonement, rejecting miracles, and rejecting the deity of Christ logically connect?

  The answers to this question may vary, but the logical connection should be clear. The rejection of miracles, for example, is a rejection of how miracles function. In the case of Jesus Christ, His miracles attested to His deity and authority, so a rejection of His miracles is a rejection of His deity. Furthermore, if Jesus were only a man, then He could not have died for the sins of another, and there would be no possibility of a substitutionary atonement.

REVIEW QUIZ

1. **B.**
Harry Emerson Fosdick was one of the prominent liberal voices in the church of Machen's day. In calling Jesus the "fairest flower of humanity," he was calling people to imitate Jesus yet not esteeming Him in His divinity.

2. **D.**
Paul stressed the importance of faith in Jesus Christ throughout his ministry. One particular text from Habakkuk 2:4 was critical to Paul's presentation of the gospel: "The righteous shall live by faith" (Rom. 1:17; Gal. 3:11).

3. **C.**
The Nicene Creed says that Jesus came "for us and for our salvation." The small prepositional phrase "for us" encapsulates the doctrine of substitutionary atonement.

4. **A.**
Even before the popularization of liberal theology in the church that Machen was attempting to correct, scholars in the nineteenth century had denied Jesus' miracles, claiming that the miracles of Jesus were embellishments created by His followers. They attempted to explain miracles such as the resurrection as a mass hallucination.

5. **B.**
Both the Nicene Creed (325) and the Chalcedonian Definition (451) address the divine and human natures of Jesus Christ, but these creedal statements do not add anything to Scripture, which clearly teaches both the divinity and the humanity of Jesus Christ.

6. **D.**
The term hypostatic union *is the technical description of how the divine and human natures of Jesus Christ subsist in one person. Christ is truly God and truly man, two natures in one person.*

11

Salvation

INTRODUCTION

The doctrine of salvation was something that liberal theologians were getting wrong, and they were corrupting the church with their teaching. Because J. Gresham Machen's *Christianity and Liberalism* is in many ways a defense of the gospel, the book builds up to its chapter on salvation. In this lesson, Dr. Nichols corrects the works-based understanding of salvation with the biblical understanding of salvation, that we are justified by faith alone in Christ alone.

LEARNING GOALS

When you have finished this lesson, you should be able to:

- Explain how our view of sin influences how we understand the gospel
- Define what occurs in God's act of justification
- Explain the nature of saving faith and what it leads to

KEY IDEAS

- Before we are justified, we stand before God as guilty and sinful people, and if we do not understand this, then we cannot comprehend the beauty of justification in the gospel.
- Saving faith understands the facts of the gospel, accepts the truth of the gospel, and trusts in Jesus Christ alone for salvation.
- Our works do not contribute to our salvation, but they do follow from our salvation.

REFLECTION & DISCUSSION QUESTIONS

Before the Video

What Do You Think?

Take a moment to answer the following questions. They will prepare you for the lecture.

- How is someone saved? What is a person saved from?

- How is your life different now than before you were a Christian?

Scripture Reading

Now we know that whatever the law says it speaks to those who are under the law, so that every mouth may be stopped, and the whole world may be held accountable to God. For by works of the law no human being will be justified in his sight, since through the law comes knowledge of sin. But now the righteousness of God has been manifested apart from the law, although the Law and the Prophets bear witness to it—the righteousness of God through faith in Jesus Christ for all who believe. For there is no distinction: for all have sinned and fall short of the glory of God, and are justified by his grace as a gift, through the redemption that is in Christ Jesus.

—Romans 3:19–24

- What is the law able to accomplish for us? How, then, must we be justified?

During the Video

Answer the following questions while you watch the video. They will guide you through the lecture.

Justification *0:00–16:21*

- What message of the opening chapters of Romans underscores the importance of justification by faith?

- What are the gospel remedies for our sinful nature and guilt?

- What were Machen's last words via telegraph before he died?

By Faith *16:21–24:25*

- How did Machen define what it means to have faith in Christ?

- What are the three elements of saving faith? What flows out of this faith?

After the Video

Answer the following questions after you have finished the lecture. They will help you identify and summarize the major points.

- At the end of the Ninety-Five Theses, Martin Luther wrote: "Away with those prophets who say, 'Peace, peace,' and there is no peace. Instead, 'Cross, cross,' and there is no cross." What does this mean, and how does it relate to Machen's context?

  If you are in a group, have the members discuss how the gospel is lost when we get wrong God's character and doctrines such as man's total depravity or moral inability.
- How does the obedience of Christ relate to the doctrine of salvation?

  If you are in a group, have the members talk about why double imputation provides Christians with a confidence to face death. Ask: How can this doctrine help you to live more faithfully right now?
- How might a Christian's living in the world and not withdrawing from it contribute to his or her sanctification?

  If you are in a group, have the members reflect on the Christian's relationship to the world. Ask: Have you ever been tempted to withdraw from ordinary life in this world? What aspects of Christian obedience would be lost if Christians were to totally withdraw from the world?

PRAYER

Commit what you have learned from God's Word in this lesson to prayer.

- Praise God for His loving character, which He displayed in sending His Son into this world.
- Confess any ways that the world might be too influential in your thoughts, words, and deeds.

- Thank God for the work of the Holy Spirit in sanctifying us even in the midst of the world.
- Ask God to enlarge your heart with the truth of the gospel so that your desire to see others experience God's love in the gospel might increase.

REVIEW QUIZ

Use these multiple-choice questions to measure what you learned from this lesson.

1. The problems that Machen addressed in liberalism's doctrine of salvation most closely correspond to the problems that were addressed in which of the following?
    a. Christian persecution of the second century
    b. Ecumenical councils of the fourth century
    c. Protestant Reformation of the sixteenth century
    d. Evangelical movement of the twentieth century
2. Paul stresses the peace with God that results from justification throughout Romans, beginning in the first chapter.
    a. True
    b. False
3. Who received the final telegraph that Machen ever sent?
    a. A.A. Hodge
    b. B.B. Warfield
    c. Charles Hodge
    d. John Murray
4. What is the most crucial element of saving faith?
    a. *Assensus*
    b. *Fiducia*
    c. *Notitia*
    d. Both a and b
5. Justification is a process that is worked out through the entirety of our lives.
    a. True
    b. False
6. Related to the lecture, what is the arena of sanctification?
    a. The heart
    b. The mind
    c. The soul
    d. The world

Answer Key—Salvation

REFLECTION & DISCUSSION QUESTIONS

Before the Video

What Do You Think?

These are personal questions. The answers should be based on your own knowledge and experience.

Scripture Reading

- What is the law able to accomplish for us? How, then, must we be justified?

  In Romans 3, Paul stresses that the law condemns us because it gives us knowledge of our sin. It helps us see that we stand in need of justification and not that justification can be attained through it, for we have all fallen short of it. It is for this reason that we need the justification that comes through Jesus Christ, who perfectly kept the law, such that faith in Him alone is the only way that we can be justified before God.

During the Video

Justification

- What message of the opening chapters of Romans underscores the importance of justification by faith?

  In Romans 1, Paul writes about the reality that the gentiles are under the wrath of God, and in Romans 2, he argues that this is the very same reality for all who have broken God's law, even the Jews who first received it in written form. In the first half of Romans 3, Paul quotes multiple passages of the Old Testament to show the extent of humanity's sinfulness. All this focus on sin is intended to set up our grave need for a way to be justified before God.

- What are the gospel remedies for our sinful nature and guilt?

  The gospel remedy for our sinful nature is regeneration, which we need to be made alive in our state of sin so that we can exercise faith through the power of the Holy Spirit. The gospel remedy for our guilt is justification, which is God's declaration of our righteousness in Jesus Christ, our sin being imputed to Him and His righteousness being imputed to us.

- What were Machen's last words via telegraph before he died?

  Machen died in 1937 on New Year's Day in North Dakota, but before he died, he sent a telegraph to John Murray, his colleague at Westminster Theological Seminary, which read: "I'm so thankful for the active obedience of Christ. No hope without it."

By Faith

- How did Machen define what it means to have faith in Christ?

  Machen defined what it means to have faith in Christ as our ceasing all attempts to win God's favor through our own efforts. Faith is ultimately in Christ alone, and we do not even place our confidence in our faith. As Machen said, "Simply resting in Christ alone, faith is the end of all our striving."

- What are the three elements of saving faith? What flows out of this faith?

  The three elements of saving faith are (1) notitia, *which is the content of the gospel in terms of its propositional facts, (2)* assensus, *which is the mental act of acknowledging the truthfulness of the content of the gospel, and (3)* fiducia, *which is the trust that we place in Christ alone. Such a faith will begin the process of sanctification, whereby we strive for holiness in the Christian life.*

After the Video

- At the end of the Ninety-Five Theses, Martin Luther wrote, "Away with those prophets who say, 'Peace, peace,' and there is no peace. Instead, 'Cross, cross,' and there is no cross." What does this mean, and how does it relate to Machen's context?

  Luther ended the Ninety-Five Theses with these words to correct the false teaching of the Roman Catholic Church. In response to the selling of indulgences, Luther rejected the teaching that people could have their unrighteousness dealt with beyond this life, attaining peace with God through purgatory or through another's purchase of indulgences for them. Luther believed that this mentality denied the cross of Jesus Christ, on which He had already died for our salvation, making people bear another type of cross that cannot save. This period of Reformation history connects to Machen's context because the false gospel of liberalism was also teaching a works-based understanding of how one can be saved.

- How does the obedience of Christ relate to the doctrine of salvation?

  Imputation is central to God's act of justification. In imputation, God reckons to our account Christ's righteousness, having reckoned our sin to Christ's account. Christ's obedience is vital to the doctrine of salvation for this reason. Christ, in His passive obedience, paid the penalty for Adam's sin and our sin. In His active obedience, Christ perfectly fulfilled the law of God. These two aspects of Christ's obedience are what makes imputation—and thus our justification—possible.

- How might a Christian's living in the world and not withdrawing from it contribute to his or her sanctification?

  Answers to this question may vary, but in Christianity and Liberalism, *Machen reminds us that we live out our sanctification as Christians in the world. We do not have the option to completely withdraw from the world. In fact, the trials that we experience in the world may actually contribute to our sanctification. If we were to remove ourselves from the world, then we might not experience the difficult circumstances that demand patient endurance or other marks of Christian character that the Spirit is happy to work out in us through them.*

REVIEW QUIZ

1. **C.**
   Ever since the age of the Apostles, the gospel has been under attack. For instance, Paul had to address the legalism of the Judaizers in Galatians. In Machen's day, liberalism was presenting another gospel of works-righteousness, and this was connected to Luther's Ninety-Five Theses and his response to the works-righteousness of Rome during the Protestant Reformation.

2. **B.**
   While Paul does open his letter to the Romans with a reflection on the gospel, he does not stress the peace that we have with God as a result of our justification in the opening chapters. Rather, in the first three chapters of the letter, he stresses that we are at war with God, everyone being under His wrath.

3. **C.**
   A.A. Hodge, B.B. Warfield, and Charles Hodge are among what is commonly referred to as "Old Princeton." John Murray also taught at Princeton Theological Seminary, but he came after the Old Princeton era. He helped found Westminster Theological Seminary with Machen and was the last person to receive a telegraph from him.

4. **B.**
   Dr. Nichols called fiducia *the "crucial piece" of faith. A person can have knowledge about the gospel, and a person may even believe that it is plausible or true, but to be saved, a person must place his or her trust fully in Jesus Christ, which is the element of faith called* fiducia.

5. **B.**
   Justification is not a process that we work through; it is an act of God whereby He declares us righteous in His sight because of the work of Jesus Christ alone. Justification does, however, lead us into the lifelong process of sanctification.

6. **D.**
   It cannot be denied that sanctification involves our whole person—body, soul, heart, and mind. There is not one part of our life that is not affected by our growth in holiness. In this lesson, however, the world was emphasized as the place that Christians work out their sanctification.

12

The Church

INTRODUCTION

Christianity and Liberalism ends with a chapter on the doctrine of the church. This was a doctrine near to J. Gresham Machen's heart. He helped form a new Presbyterian denomination in hopes that the church would remain pure in its teaching, and he founded a new theological seminary so that ministers would be thoroughly trained to edify the church. In this lesson, Dr. Nichols concludes this series by helping us see that the church has the same calling today as it did in Machen's day.

LEARNING GOALS

When you have finished this lesson, you should be able to:

- Identify Machen's central convictions about the church's identity and calling
- Describe why the church ought to be confident in the face of change and even adversity
- Explain how the church can provide answers to its surrounding culture

KEY IDEAS

- Machen held the conviction that believers are united in the church through the cross and that ministers need to serve the church with creedal integrity.
- We ought to reflect on God's promises to the church, and to His people who are the church, to remain faithful in a changing world.
- The church can fulfill its mission to the world only through the proclamation of the gospel.

REFLECTION & DISCUSSION QUESTIONS

Before the Video

What Do You Think?

Take a moment to answer the following questions. They will prepare you for the lecture.

- Why is belonging to a church important?

- What should characterize the preaching of the church?

Scripture Reading

I therefore, a prisoner for the Lord, urge you to walk in a manner worthy of the calling to which you have been called, with all humility and gentleness, with patience, bearing with one another in love, eager to maintain the unity of the Spirit in the bond of peace. There is one body and one Spirit—just as you were called to the one hope that belongs to your call—one Lord, one faith, one baptism, one God and Father of all, who is over all and through all and in all. But grace was given to each one of us according to the measure of Christ's gift. . . . And he gave the apostles, the prophets, the evangelists, the shepherds and teachers, to equip the saints for the work of ministry, for building up the body of Christ, until we all attain to the unity of the faith and of the knowledge of the Son of God.

—Ephesians 4:1–7, 11–13

- What major theme is seen throughout this passage? How are ministers Christ's gift to the church? How might they be faithful to their calling?

During the Video

Answer the following questions while you watch the video. They will guide you through the lecture.

Ministering with Integrity *0:00–8:24*

- Why is it fitting that a chapter on the doctrine of the church should follow the chapter on the doctrine of salvation in *Christianity and Liberalism*?

- In addition to the cross, what else did Machen believe the church centers on? Why is this conviction a part of Machen's response to liberalism?

Our Faithful God *8:24–15:10*

- What was the trend at General Assembly from 1915 to 1930?

- What two things does Machen remind his readers of, despite this trend?

The Church as the Church *15:10–24:39*

- What is the wrong way for the church to go about answering cultural upheaval?

- What is the business of the church?

After the Video

Answer the following questions after you have finished the lecture. They will help you identify and summarize the major points.

- What happens when the church imitates the culture? Have you ever seen this play out in your experience?

  If you are in a group, have the members discuss the potential benefits that the church might have in existing in a world that continually embraces darkness in its rejection of the light of truth.
- How do the two promises of God that Machen reminds us of in *Christianity and Liberalism* go hand in hand?

  If you are in a group, have the members read Matthew 16:13–20. Ask: Seeing one of these promises of God in context, how does this promise support Machen's conviction that ministers must serve with creedal integrity?
- Explain the purpose of Dr. Nichols' description of the Palace Beautiful from John Bunyan's *The Pilgrim's Progress.*

  If you are in a group, have the members reflect on and discuss the most significant things that they have learned from this teaching series.

PRAYER

Commit what you have learned from God's Word in this lesson to prayer.

- Praise God for His power to fulfill all His promises for His people and His church.
- Confess any feelings of despair about the state of the world and the church that are not rooted in faith.
- Thank God that He has promised in Christ that the gates of hell shall not prevail against the church.
- Ask God to preserve your church in the faithful preaching of the gospel.

REVIEW QUIZ

Use these multiple-choice questions to measure what you learned from this lesson.

1. Which is the "forgotten standard" among the Westminster Standards?
   a. Westminster Confession of Faith
   b. Westminster Larger Catechism
   c. Westminster Shorter Catechism
   d. Westminster Directory of Public Worship

2. Machen was unsympathetic toward ministers who wavered on their doctrinal convictions, yet he was pastorally concerned for ordinary Christians who had doubts.
   a. True
   b. False

3. What key term summarizes Machen's conviction about the church in relation to the fidelity of its ministers?
   a. Creedal guardian
   b. Establishmentarian
   c. Pasture of Christ's sheep
   d. Voluntary association

4. What Old Testament figure did Machen allude to as illustrative of the church?
   a. Abraham
   b. Elijah
   c. Jeremiah
   d. Moses

5. The growth of moderates among the Presbyterian denomination contributed to the decline of conservatives in key positions from 1915 to 1930.
   a. True
   b. False

6. Which of the following promises from Scripture do *not* relate to the two promises of God that Machen reassured us of in *Christianity and Liberalism*?
   a. "I will build my church, and the gates of hell shall not prevail against it" (Matt. 16:18).
   b. "I should lose nothing of all that he [the Father] has given me [Jesus]" (John 6:39).
   c. "I, when I am lifted up from the earth, will draw all people to myself" (John 12:32).
   d. "God is faithful, and he will not let you be tempted beyond your ability" (1 Cor. 10:13).

Answer Key—The Church

REFLECTION & DISCUSSION QUESTIONS

Before the Video

What Do You Think?

These are personal questions. The answers should be based on your own knowledge and experience.

Scripture Reading

- What major theme is seen throughout this passage? How are ministers Christ's gift to the church? How might they be faithful to their calling?

  Paul urges the Ephesians to unity throughout this passage, making appeals to the one body, one Spirit, one hope, one Lord, one faith, one baptism, and one God and Father, all of which provide the basis of our Christian unity. Ministers are called to build up the church as the one body of Christ for the work of ministry, and they can be faithful to this only if they are teaching the one faith, the one body of teaching that is given to us in Scripture.

During the Video

Ministering with Integrity

- Why is it fitting that a chapter on the doctrine of the church should follow the chapter on the doctrine of salvation in *Christianity and Liberalism*?

  The chapters of Christianity and Liberalism *follow a logical order. The logical connection between the last two chapters is that salvation is unto something. When Jesus saves us, He brings us into union not only with God but also with other Christians. He unites us to His body, the church.*

- In addition to the cross, what else did Machen believe the church centers on? Why is this conviction a part of Machen's response to liberalism?

  The church centers on the cross because it is centered on the gospel and Jesus Christ. It is His body. The church also centers on a creed. Dr. Nichols used this term to summarize the doctrinal conviction of the church, especially among its ministers. Machen stressed this because liberal ministers were breaking their ministerial vows in not teaching the theology of the Westminster Standards. He believed that these ministers ought to be faithful to their vows or, because the church is a voluntary association, take their teaching elsewhere.

Our Faithful God

- What was the trend at General Assembly from 1915 to 1930?

  From 1915 to 1930, the conservative influence within the Presbyterian denomination was waning, and conservative ministers were no longer holding key positions on denominational committees. This was due to the rise of liberals and moderates within the denomination.

- What two things does Machen remind his readers of, despite this trend?

  In Christianity and Liberalism, *Machen gives the encouragement that God has not deserted His church. In fact, Machen believed that God was doing something new, since "the darkest hour has always come before the dawn." Machen also gives the encouragement that God continues to use the church to bring people to Himself.*

The Church as the Church

- What is the wrong way for the church to go about answering cultural upheaval?

  Machen identified a problem in Christianity and Liberalism, *that churches were becoming less like the church and more like the world. The church was imitating the culture. This is the wrong way to go about providing answers to societal problems.*

- What is the business of the church?

  The best way for the church to provide answers to societal problems is to remain the church, being faithful to its proclamation of Jesus Christ. This is what Dr. Nichols called "the business of the church" in line with Machen: "The business of the church is to proclaim, to preach Jesus Christ and Him crucified."

After the Video

- What happens when the church imitates the culture? Have you ever seen this play out in your experience?

  The answer to the second question is personal, and answers may vary. As for the first question, when the church imitates the culture, it cannot be distinguished from the culture. It will cease to be the "house of God" and the "gate of heaven." It will not be able to provide the refreshment and nourishment that is found only in Christ.

- How do the two promises of God that Machen reminds us of in *Christianity and Liberalism* go hand in hand?

  The two promises that God has not deserted His church and that the church will continue to be used to draw people to Himself go together because the church is made up of the people of God. As long as God is calling His elect to Himself, the church as we know it as an earthly institution will exist and must remain faithful in preaching the gospel of Jesus Christ that God uses to save His people.

- Explain the purpose of Dr. Nichols' description of the Palace Beautiful from John Bunyan's *The Pilgrim's Progress.*

  In Bunyan's The Pilgrim's Progress, *the Palace Beautiful is the place where Christian, weary from his journey, finds rest. It is a house of refreshment that was built by the Lord. But before he entered this house, he needed to be interviewed, which pictures for us the process that many of us have gone through in becoming members of a church. After professing his faith, Christian is nourished, just as we are by the preached Word of God, and he is given rest and outfitted to go into the world. This is the vision of the church that Dr. Nichols wanted to convey in these poetic terms, so that we would see its beauty and place in our lives.*

REVIEW QUIZ

1. **D.**
   The Westminster Directory of Public Worship is what Dr. Nichols identified as the "forgotten standard" of the Westminster Standards. It is a document that outlines different elements of a worship service that is seldom used by churches despite the enduring legacy of the Westminster Confession of Faith and Larger and Shorter Catechisms.

2. **A.**
   Machen was against the idea that ministers would vow to uphold the teaching of the Westminster Standards and yet deny central doctrines of the Christian faith that are contained within it. He did, on the other hand, care for people who had sincere questions about their faith, which is perhaps why he did not tolerate ministers who could not give the biblical answers to these questions.

3. **D.**
   Machen called the church a "voluntary association." He did not mean that things such as church membership and attending worship are optional. Rather, he meant that the ministers who served the church, if they found their doctrine out of accord with the teaching of the church, should feel the freedom to teach according to their consciences elsewhere.

4. **B.**
   As the church, sometimes we can feel as though, with the trends in culture and even within the church itself, we are the only ones who are faithful. This is why Elijah was alluded to. In a time of apostasy in Israel, he thought that he stood alone for the Lord, but the Lord assured him that there were seven thousand Israelites who had not bowed the knee to the false god Baal.

5. **A.**
   Not only were liberals influencing the Presbyterian denomination in such a way that conservative voices were not being heard in important positions, but also the moderates within the church were increasing, allowing liberalism a stronger foothold.

6. **D.**
The two promises that Machen encourages us with in Christianity and Liberalism *are that God has not deserted His church and is using it to continue to call people to Himself. The only promise that does not deal explicitly with God's preservation of the church and His saving His people is "God is faithful, and he will not let you be tempted beyond your ability" (1 Cor. 10:13).*